Foreword

Whenever I find any confusion in my mind about educational matters, I turn to two sources to help me out. One is John Holt and his ten books on education, and the other is the writings of Bertrand Russell, especially his two books on education.

Russell challenges many current dogmas of education. Take, for example, the present obsession with competition in and around education. Russell is not impressed: *"Competition is not only bad as an educational fact, but also as a ideal to be held before the young. What the world now needs is not competition but organisation and co-operation; all belief in the utility of competition has become an anachronism. ... the emotions connected with it are the emotions of hostility and ruthlessness. The conception of society as an organic whole is very difficult for those whose minds have been steeped in competitive ideas. Ethically, therefore, no less than economically, it is undesirable to teach the young to be competitive."*

Russell would have been antagonistic to the idea of a National Curriculum: *" ... much education consists in the instilling of unfounded dogmas in the place of a spirit of inquiry. This results, not necessarily from any fault in the teacher, but from a curriculum which demands too much apparent knowledge, with a consequent need of haste and undue definiteness."*

You are not free without good habits, Russell argued, for you become enslaved to bad habits. Erratic sleep habits, junk food diets, smoking and drug addiction provide obvious examples, but Russell applied this to study as well: *"If curiosity is to be fruitful, it must be associated with a certain technique for the acquistion of knowledge. There must be habits of observation, belief in the possibility of knowledge, patience and industry."*

Another good habit was happiness. Not only did Russell write a book entitled *The Conquest of Happiness*, but he saw it as essential basis both for learning and the health of society: *"Happiness in childhood is absolutely necessary to the production of the best type of human being."*

Over-teaching, on the other hand, was another bad habit: *"If personal quality is to be preserved, definite teaching must be reduced to a minimum, and criticism must never be carried to such lengths as to produce timidity in self-expression. But these maxims are not likely to lead to work that will be pleasing to an inspector."*

Russell had a radical vision of officials that is hard to find in our domination-riddled mass schooling system and its endless supply of control-freaks: *"The administrator of the future must be the servant of free citizens, not the benevolent ruler of admiring subjects."*

It is high time we revisited the educational writings of Bertrand Russell, and when I sought someone to do this service for us, the name of Chris Shute was top of the list. Happily, he accepted the challenge and this splendid short book is the result.

Roland Meighan

Bertrand Russell:

'education as the power of independent thought'

by **Chris Shute**

Published 2002 by Educational Heretics Press
113 Arundel Drive, Bramcote Hills, Nottingham NG9 3FQ

British Cataloguing in Publication Data

Shute, Chris
   Bertrand Russell: 'education as the power of
   independent thought'
   1. Russell, Bertrand, 1872-1970 – Contributions
   in education
   2.Education – Philosophy
   I.Title
   370.1

ISBN 1-900219-21-2

Design and production: Educational Heretics Press

Cover design Annabel Toogood

Printed by Mastaprint Plus Ltd., Sandiacre, Nottm. NG10 5AH
Telephone: 0115 939 1772

Contents

Dedication

To my dear mother,

who doesn't really know if she approves of this sort of thing.

Loan Receipt
Liverpool John Moores University
Library Services

Borrower Name: Hegarty, Aoife
EDNAHEG1
Borrower ID: ********

Bertrand Russell, "education as the power
of independent thought" /
31111010782074
Due Date: 30/11/2018 23:59:00 GMT

Total Items: 1
3/11/2018 16:02

Chapter one

Bertrand Russell
- an educator ahead of his time

Introduction

Many people who have no particular reason for knowing anything about Bertrand Russell's life and thought, have at least one memory of him: a man almost impossibly old, with a sharp-featured, bird-like head, sitting in the road amidst C.N.D banners, waiting for the police to carry him away. That image characterised him admirably because it showed him as what he certainly was at heart, not a rebel for rebellion's sake, but a man who, when the world around him seemed to have parted company with reason and good moral sense, saw no virtue in following it down that path.

I came late to Bertrand Russell's work, and I confess I found him a daunting subject for study. Almost uniquely among first-rank thinkers he addressed himself to audiences as widely disparate as Victorian England and Cold-War America. His work in education was radical enough to bring him into contact with A.S.Neill of Summerhill, but his own childhood had included being shown round Rugby School by his cousin, Dean Stanley, who had provided the inspiration for the character of George Arthur, the saintly schoolboy in *Tom Brown's Schooldays*. Though his own education had been almost entirely in the hands of tutors, he founded a school, Beacon Hill. It failed, as radical schools often do, because it could not attract enough pupils, and those who did come had parents who did not always pay their bills. He found that, like A.S.Neill, he was able to cure children with emotional problems, but not to persuade their parents to leave their youngsters with him when they had become more manageable. Talking about his educational ideas, therefore, is always likely to attract the criticism that he was no more than a crank who let his pupils do as they liked, and encouraged them to dance naked and be atheists.

Such disparities are, of course, capable of being seen from another angle. Anyone who hopes to change education for the better must be willing to think of childhood in ways which differ from the common standard. Our culture surrounds childhood with a strange rag-bag of feelings, superficially rational, but ultimately generated in the deepest parts of our collective psyche. Because we are modern people, who assume that they have thrown off the chains of superstition and arbitrary power, we feel that what we do to our children is sensible, and 'for their own good', but on closer examination it is possible to conclude that, although much has changed for the better in the externals of education, in its fundamentals it is still a way of dragooning children into our tribal mores without their having thought seriously and critically about them. We are generally self-confident enough not to dread, as many immigrant families do, the loss of essential parts of our way of life, but we still see our children as dangerous people who may 'let us down', or 'be naughty' unless we lay down the law to them, and ensure that they never act independently of our will for them until they become adults. So we make them, if not our slaves, then at the very least our chattels, with only one responsibility - to become exactly like us. Russell rejected that culturally conditioned view of education, as I do, because it is dangerous to mankind and fundamentally inhumane.

Russell did not receive a conventional education. His mind was formed not by schoolmasters in classrooms but by tutors. Some of them were German, and he learned to speak their language, absorbing at the same time ideas about mathematics and philosophy which were to become the basis of his life's work. It may be said with certainty that his childhood was as far as it is possible to imagine from the experience of ordinary youngsters growing up in Britain during the last half of Victoria's reign. Yet his privileged early years, free as they were from the influence of harsh, authoritarian teaching and a rigid curriculum, allowed him to see with unique clarity how growing minds can be smothered and their ability to think largely destroyed by being made to adjust to a regime of enforced learning. That regime produced the vast majority of the people who theorise about education, and then organise it on the basis of that theorising. Russell was one of the very few educational thinkers who could see what lay outside the palisade that tradition always erects around itself, ostensibly to keep evil influences out, but in reality to preserve its own dominance, and to ward off dangerous changes.

At the very beginning of his autobiography, Russell set out the essence of his life's work:

> "*Three passions, simple but overwhelmingly strong, have governed my life: the longing for love, the search for knowledge, and unbearable pity for the suffering of mankind".*
>
> (The Autobiography of Bertrand Russell, Prologue)

Comment on his love-life, which was varied and not without drama, would be out of place in this book, but the latter two concerns are intimately bound up with education. I shall try to show in this book that Russell believed in learning as a lifelong pursuit, from which no-one should be excluded by any factor which could be controlled and eliminated from their life. Because he avoided the experience of school himself he was able to separate in his mind the formal process of indoctrination which most children go through and the disinterested satisfaction of healthy curiosity which is the natural token of man's intellectual superiority over all other animals. As he wrote in his major analysis of education:

> "*The spontaneous wish to learn, which every normal child possesses, as shown in its efforts to walk and talk, should be the driving force in education.*"   (On Education, p.25)

Having worked in schools for most of my adult life, I should like to have the power to cause that sentence to be inscribed on the back wall of every classroom in the land. It expresses the core of Russell's thinking about children's needs, and it would give deep offence to the many enemies of spontaneity who seem to rise to the heights of influence in traditional education. In spite of their perpetual failure to create an education system from which everyone emerges into adulthood sane, curious, sociable and with their minds well-furnished with strong, healthy ideas and a rich culture, the 'back-to-basics' people still reign supreme over the experience of childhood. The simplistic policy-makers who judge the content of children's learning not by the youngsters' enthusiasm for it, but by the stress and boredom it creates in them, even now hold and almost unchallenged patent for the practice of education, and by the sheer weight of received ideas it forces them to imbibe. Russell saw that this was an endemic symptom of the kind of education states organise for their young, and he denounced it firmly:

"We are faced with the paradoxical fact that education has become one of the chief obstacles to intelligence and freedom of thought."   (On Education, p.28)

My intention in writing this book is not simply to expound Russell's ideas: that has already been done by others, such as Joe Park (*Bertrand Russell on Education*, Allen and Unwin, 1964). In any case, Russell's own words are clear and engaging. Rather, I hope to respond dynamically to his approach to education, recognising and pointing out from my own experience the truth of his analysis, and showing - as far as any individual can - that his ideas are more than simply a part of a larger body of intellectual work which is admired from afar, but never allowed to get in the way of ordinary thinking and the organisation of everyday life.

Russell often used anecdotes from his daily life to illustrate the development of his understanding of children. He believed that education in general and parental work in particular tended to be successful to the extent that they were based on the careful observation of children. My own experience, as a teacher and an educator, leads me to agree. Adults often assume that they 'understand' children merely because they have themselves grown up and finished with childhood. They suppose that their adult status entitles them to decide what children need and how they should be made to think. This leads to incessant conflict, and the progressive sapping of children's self-confidence to the point where they no longer believe that they can do anything for themselves, or know anything valuable unless an adult has intervened to 'validate' it.

As a result of such insensitivity, we see vast numbers of schoolchildren leaving school without ever having felt in control of their learning, or of the course of their life. Then we give them the vote, expect them to make sensible decisions, and play a full part in our national life. This seems to me, as I suspect it would have appeared to Russell, as little more enlightened than expecting a person to learn to swim without ever entering a body of water. By referring to real incidents, both in Russell's experience and my own, I hope to show that good educational thought, which leads to genuine maturity in adult life, can only come from seeing and responding to what children honestly feel and wish to do for themselves.

Why write about Russell?

I have often noticed, with amazement and frustration, that English education is, in fact, not a particularly intellectual business. When universal schooling started it was bright working-class youngsters who learned the scraps of knowledge their masters thought to be somehow 'basic' or 'essential', and then spent a lifetime being paid a pittance to hand that knowledge on to their fellows. They were not expected to think much about the needs or the psychology of their pupils, who, in any case, came before them in such enormous classes that they could only do their job with even a modicum of success if they adopted a rigid teaching style which stifled any interaction with individual children except when the teacher specifically allowed it. Despite the vast improvements which have taken place in teacher training and the culture of the classroom, despite the broadening of the curriculum and the opening of the gates of higher education to more and more young people, grinding away under the surface of even the most modern school is a folk-memory which expresses itself through some variant of the advice proffered to me on my first day as a teacher by the head of geography: *"Now look here, sonny, forget all that high-falutin' stuff you learned at college. The only way to succeed in this business is to hold them down and make them work."* I cannot be certain of the words, but the message is exact.

It was made clear to me that control was everything, and the more abstract arts of psychology and pedagogy had to fit in wherever the grim business of crushing dissent and scaring knowledge into the young allowed them to. This often meant not at all.

I have told the tale of how I discarded that idea of my role in education in another book (*Compulsory Schooling Disease*). Since leaving teaching I have come to see that the State system has become dangerously impoverished precisely because it limits its vision to the nineteenth century idea that all children need to be dragged into classrooms and stuffed with undigested and disjointed knowledge. It cannot allow teachers and pupils to pursue learning in their own chosen rhythm, because to do so would interrupt the 'delivery' of the curriculum, the whole curriculum and nothing but the curriculum, which has become the sole purpose of schooling, as much now as it was in the late 1800s.

This bleak culture cannot easily give rise to progressive thought, still less to progressive action. If we look at it with rigour and detachment we quickly see that it is incapable of giving children the intellectual and social grounding they need, except by sheer accident.

When we look at the more accessible works of Bertrand Russell we find ourselves examining the world in which we live through the eyes of a person who saw no reason to sanctify existing ideas, not because they had no value at all, but rather because no-one had ever thought it necessary to tell him that he could not challenge them.

During his early years Russell had the run of Pembroke Lodge, a fine rambling house in Richmond Park, given to his grandparents by Queen Victoria. I have visited it many times - it is now a teahouse - and I share with him a sense of the great value to children of being allowed to play in wild surroundings, where there are:

> " ... *summerhouses, sweet briar hedges, thickets of laurel, and all kinds of secret places in which it was possible to hide from grown-up people so successfully that there was not the slightest fear of discovery.*"
>
> (The Autobiography of Bertrand Russell, p.14)

From there, Russell went to a 'Crammer', an intensive academic course designed to prepare him for a Cambridge Scholarship. He was only fifteen at the time, and was working in a traditional classroom for the first time in his life. He was teased, partly because his response to the rowdy adolescent horseplay which heralded the development of sexual feelings in his fellow students was to withdraw from them and commune with himself as much as possible. A traditional commentator on education might be tempted to suggest that this response to teenage noisiness was good evidence that he had lost out socially by being educated at home. In fact, he does not seem to have been as deeply affected by it as many children are. Perhaps he had had time to build a good positive image of himself, which protected him from the deeper scars which bullying often produces. Nonetheless, he admits in his

Autobiography to having been very unhappy, even at times suicidal. He did not kill himself, he wrote:

> " ... *because I wished to know more of mathematics. My people would, of course, have been horrified if they had known of the sort of conversation that was habitual, but as I was getting on well with mathematics I wished on the whole to stay, and never told them a word as to the sort of place it was.* "   (Autobiography, p.38)

It is noticeable that even at 15, Russell was able to balance the strength of his intellectual needs with the undoubtedly corrosive surroundings in which he was obliged to satisfy them. I have rarely met this clarity of intent in schooled children, though one of my younger friends who was educated at home once remarked to me that although he was afraid of the English tutor who was preparing him for GCSE, and disliked his whole manner and personality, he was learning from him, and so would not stop having lessons with him. I suspect that it is mainly people who have had a chance to manage their own learning who develop such a measure of self-control.

Russell was deeply committed to the pursuit of reason. As a youth he wrote:

> "*In all things I have made the vow to follow reason, not the instincts inherited partly from my ancestors and gained gradually by them, owing to a process of natural selection, and partly due to my education. How absurd it would be to follow these in the questions of right and wrong. For, as I observed before, the inherited part can only be principles leading to the preservation of the species to which I belong, the part due to education is good or bad according to the individual education. Yet this inner voice, this God-given conscience which made Bloody Mary burn the Protestants, this is what we reasonable beings are to follow. I think this idea mad and I endeavour to go by reason as far as possible. What I take as my ideal is that which ultimately produces (the) greatest happiness of (the) greatest number. Then I can apply reason to find out the course most conducive to this end.*"   (Autobiography, p.47)

No-one, not even the thinker Russell was, can sustain this position throughout every second of their life, but as a general principle this is an admirable standpoint for an educator. It is worth remarking that the appeal to reason is not popular in modern educational thinking, partly because children and how we treat them are visceral rather than cerebral issues. Our governors do not normally draw up their plans for educating children after studying their real needs. It is the needs and aspirations of their parents which determine the national ethos of education, and these are generally as far from the exercise of reason as it is possible to imagine. Regrettably, education is always based primarily on what the Government thinks adults will vote for.

Russell's message to the world of education is, in simple terms, look at children and try to determine, in concert with them, what their minds are leading them to do and what knowledge they are keen to acquire. Then you will find in them not dogged opponents and committed rebels, but happy fellow-travellers along the path which leads to a fulfilled life.

Education and the Social Order

A certain way of educating people thrust itself onto the stage of history on 11th September 2001. I suspect that this will become one of the few dates that most people can quote from memory. They may even remember that it was a Tuesday. Two hijacked airliners plunged into the World Trade Centre in New York, a third dived into the Pentagon and a fourth, presumably because some of its passengers intervened, crashed without damaging any buildings. The two towers of the World Trade Centre caught fire and then, unexpectedly, crashed to the ground, killing without discrimination office workers, policemen, firemen and rescue workers.

At the time I write this nothing is known for certain about the motives of the young men who caused the catastrophe. They were assumed to be Muslim extremists, since their given names on the passenger manifest of the aircraft they seized were Arabic. They died with their hostages in an act of self-immolation so bizarre and baffling that the civilised world has not yet found a context in which to think about it. It cannot be called cowardice, since they did what they did knowing that they could not hope to escape death themselves. Neither would it be right to describe it as heroism: to die while killing others might be seen as admirable in war, if those others were enemy soldiers, engaged in combat, but these hostages were entirely innocent, thrust into the horror of their death by the most random of occurrences - having bought a ticket for a doomed flight. The murderous determination of the young terrorists seems to have had a religious dynamic, yet no major religion, including their own, Islam, actually commands its believers to kill innocent people merely because they belong to a certain nation. In short, this catastrophe, which will affect the whole world's outlook on life for many years to come, does not fit into exactly any existing category of actions. It happened because a group of people shared angry feelings and a conviction that their anger pleased their God and authorised them to act as they did.

The world urgently needs to know where these homicidal thoughts come from. I contend, and I feel entitled to suggest that Bertrand Russell would agree with me, that they were the natural outcome of a specific process of education, managed by teachers who soberly set out to make their young students think of self-immolation as the best possible goal for their lives. That process was not characterised by a specific religion: Islam is not more likely than any other faith to produce murderers. Nor did it have much to do with the language, the customs or the rituals of the country where it took place. The young murderers happen to have been Arabs, but the sad history of such acts includes people from most religions and none at all, as well as natives of most countries, both those reckoned 'civilised' and those whose way of life we in the West call 'primitive'.

The horror of the Twin Towers was, I suggest, the product of a way of relating to people when they are young which they take into themselves without understanding its power, and transform into a model of human virtue from which they feel unable to detach themselves in later life. Even when the behaviours it produces are clearly inhumane and even brutal, the mere fact that childhood experience was inescapable and all-encompassing makes it almost impossible for the young people who lived through it to recognise its character and distance themselves from it.

In this book I hope to find some clues to creating a form of education which does not overwhelm and destroy the natural goodness and common-sense which children often display in its purest form when they are very young. I want to show that

Bertrand Russell, for all the distortions which have accumulated round the common image of him as a utopian leftie whose thinking was so elevated that it did not touch the life of ordinary people, understood what mankind needs in order to survive, and spoke clearly and simply about how we can transmit that understanding to the coming generations.

Bertrand Russell, though he lived much of his life in more tranquil times, was quite certain that the genesis of evils like the World Trade Centre outrage could be recognised and understood if society could only be persuaded to look critically at its arrangements for educating children. Despite the appearance of change which he saw in British education during his lifetime he was convinced that:

> " ... *education in the modern world tends to be a reactionary force, supporting the government when it is conservative and opposing it when it is progressive. Unfortunately, also, the elements of good citizenship which are emphasised in schools are the worst elements and not the best. What is emphasised most of all is patriotism in a somewhat militant form: that is to say, a narrow devotion to the persons living in a chosen area, as opposed to those living elsewhere, and willingness to further the interests of the persons in the chosen area by the use of military force.*"
>
> (Education and the Social Order, p.15)

These ideas were in part a response to the First World War. He had been imprisoned for his campaigning against conscription. He had been horrified by the ease with which whole populations of young men could be convinced that their duty called upon them to leave their homes, families, work and communities and throw themselves into a war from which they could not benefit in any way against an enemy for whom they had no sense of personal hatred. He recognised that only people who have not learned to think for themselves can be easily and effectively drawn into realising the grandiose projects of tyrants and chauvinists, and he wanted reforms in education to bring more and more young people into adulthood with the courage and vision to follow the path in life which they know to be right for them, as long as it harms no-one else. As he put it in *Education and the Social Order*:

> "*I do not believe that a free education need make a boy or girl incapable of kindly manners, not of that degree of*

external decorum which conventional life demands. Nor do I
believe that the pain of conformity after a free education is
nearly so great as the pain caused by the complexes which
are implanted in the course of a conventional education ...
Our world contains grave evils, which can be remedied if
men wish to remedy them. Those who are aware of these evils
and fight against them are likely, it is true, to have less
everyday happiness than those who acquiesce in the status
quo. *But in place of everyday happiness they will have*
something which I, for my part, value more highly, both for
myself and for my children. They will have the sense of doing
what lies in their power to make the world less painful."
(Education and the Social Order, pp. 63-4)

So, Russell saw clearly that education played a determining role in
forming the general character of each generation. He also observed
that the theory which governed education in any age marked the
generation which had to submit to it in important ways. He felt that
there were three major theories behind educational thinking. They
were divergent, and at times contradictory.

" ... the first considers that the sole purpose of education is to
provide opportunities of growth and to remove hampering
influences. The second holds that the purpose of education is
to give culture to the individual and to develop his capacities
to the utmost. The third holds that education is to be
considered rather in relation to the community than in
relation to the individual, and that its business is to train
useful citizens."   (Education and the Social Order . p.21)

Modern education mostly seems to pursue the third set of aims: we
hear much about the teaching of 'Citizenship', the assumption
being that schools have a role which goes far beyond mere
instruction. They are expected to make their pupils good, and
teach them to be 'orderly' and compliant, like the good subjects
which the Law deems them to be. Russell insisted that all three
theories needed to be balanced, and that the preponderance of one
over the others led inevitably to bad and disruptive behaviours.
Modern educators like to think their influence is beneficent and
liberal, but they are constricted in their thinking by the fact that
they are expected to be what the mass of the voters believe that a
'good' teacher is. Since most people, even in 21st Century Britain,
think that the main purpose of 'good' teachers is to show children

that life is often unpleasant, and that they must not expect everything to happen as they wish it to, the education system which adults will vote for is unlikely to correspond very closely to that which reason suggests is best.

Russell inveighed against compulsion in education. He was not entirely alone in this, but his belief that freedom was inseparable from good education was one not often shared in an age when compulsion was the lifeblood of government at all levels.

> " ... compulsion in education ... destroys originality and intellectual interest. Desire for knowledge, at any rate for a good deal of knowledge, is natural to the young, but is generally destroyed by the fact that they are given more than they desire or can assimilate. Children who are forced to eat acquire a loathing for food, and children who are forced to learn acquire a loathing for knowledge."
> (Education and the Social Order, p.23)

As a Society we need to recognise the truth of this observation, because, as Russell foresaw, by forcing knowledge down children's throats for more than a century we have certainly created several generations of philistines, incapable of enjoying more than a tiny part of our national culture, bored in a midst of ever-increasing sources of interest and diversion, and often anti-social because their own experience as children leads them to expect that when they grow up they will have to compete in a cut-throat struggle for recognition and the exercise of power over others.

Chapter two

Russell and children

In a lifetime of work with children I have noticed that, in the West at least, children are assumed to be whatever an adult says they are. If I say that a certain child is 'being naughty' I am allowed to punish them, or at least to be angry with them. It may be that the youngster is doing something that children do naturally - running, shouting, fidgeting, making noise - but if I decide that in my code of ethics (which is often malleable and closely related to my own state of mind), the kid is at fault, I am allowed to intervene and do something about it. The only restriction on my freedom to do this is the child's own parent, who might be inclined to support me, but might equally decide that 'disciplining' their children is their business and no-one else's. In neither case, however, would any attention be paid to what the child was actually feeling, or to their real intentions and motives. Russell, who was a scientist and applied the methods of science to everything he thought about, believed that no-one could educate a child without observing very rigorously that child's behaviour.

He began, naturally with his own children. As he watched them grow up he realised that the accepted pattern of what is wrongly called 'discipline' was profoundly unhelpful to most children. He stigmatised it in his book *On Education*:

> " ... *The old idea of 'discipline' was simple. A child or boy was ordered to do something he disliked, or abstain from something he liked. When he disobeyed he suffered physical chastisement, or, in extreme cases, solitary confinement on bread and water.*"

He goes on to recount an episode from a nineteenth century novel aimed at the Moral Improvement of Children, *The Fairchild Family*, in which a son is taught Latin in order that he might become a clergyman. When he refuses to apply himself as earnestly as his father wishes he is shut up in an attic with only bread and water and forbidden to speak to anyone. Such treatment would be punished in our times, but it was seen as proper in the Victorian era, because it gave expression to the almost universal conviction that children are lazy and weak-willed, and cannot achieve anything without pressure from the outside. In contrast to such barbarisms, Russell noticed that his son, whom he sent to a Montessori school at the age of three, seemed to be becoming more disciplined and sociable, in spite of the fact that Madame Montessori was generally reckoned to have done away with external discipline. He noticed that the little boy seemed to accept such rules as there were in his class willingly, and in the same spirit that he accepted the rules of playground games. They were the means by which he got pleasure out of life in his nursery. Russell clearly perceived, as many do not even today, that to hate imposed control and direction is essentially a healthy reaction, whether in a child or an adult. He was not concerned that his son would become 'disobedient' or rebellious, because he understood that when the boy was confronted with an activity which he wanted to do he would submit happily to its strictures, and if his surroundings were conducive to positive activity and enjoyable experience the unavoidable restrictions that go with living in any community would not dull his pleasure in living.

I have seen some youngsters brought up in surroundings not unlike the Montessori class Russell's boy attended. They were not schooled, but brought up by their parents. I, who had been a schoolteacher for twenty-five years, had expected them to find study difficult, since they had done very little of the usual range of subject-work during their first 12 years. I found to my astonishment, however, that when they felt the time had come for them to start seriously preparing for their future lives, that they put aside play and settled down to absorbing, in a matter of months, the knowledge they had decided they needed for their careers. One of them said to me, without any particular emotion, that he did not like the subjects he was studying, but accepted that no-one would take him seriously if he did not have exam passes in them. Both he and his brother went on to become successful computer technicians.

Russell would not, I think, have been surprised to see youngsters like these growing up without formal schooling. He always laid great stress on the environment in which children grow up as the main defining influence on their lives. He held that, at the beginning of their lives, children have 'reflexes and instincts, but no habits'. During their earliest years their parents have, he believed a golden opportunity to create in them habits which will make them become 'the sort of person who will be liked and will be able to cope with life successfully'. Unlike, perhaps, some more modern and radical educational theorists, he held that even in the earliest moments of life children had a capacity to acquire 'bad' habits: if crying produced 'agreeable' results for the infant, he or she would, he thought, carry on crying. This querulous insistence upon having one's needs met could become part of the adult's character, making him or her a tireless complainer who risked being disliked without knowing why. This approach to childhood may give unconscious expression to the enormously powerful influence which Russell's Victorian upbringing exerted upon him, even as he worked to establish a new, more liberal understanding of what it was to be a human being. He resisted the Christian belief that children were basically flawed and sinful, needing to be 'corrected' by harsh punishment and physical suffering. Yet we find him saying:

> *"Every educated mother nowadays knows such simple facts as the importance of feeding the infant at regular intervals, not whenever it cries. This practice has arisen because it is better for the child's digestion, which is an entirely sufficient reason. But it is also desirable from the point of view of moral education. Infants are far more cunning (not in the American sense) than grown-up people are apt to suppose; if they find that crying produces agreeable results, they will cry."* (On Education, p.60)

It is, perhaps, strange to see the apostle of freedom and humanism in the same school of thought as Dr. Truby King, who condemned a generation of babies to mechanistic child-rearing based on the rhythm of the clock and the strict regulation of motherly love.

On the other hand, Russell had no doubt that children would be better off being brought up by people who valued their spontaneity, and recognised that healthy children needed to have a strong sense that the world was there to be explored and used. There would certainly have to be limits to that activity, and Russell rejected any idea that parents should be tyrannised by their children's insatiable demands.

> *"The right rule is: encourage spontaneous activities, but discourage demands upon others. Do not let the child see how much you do for it, or how much trouble you take. Let it, wherever possible, taste the joy of a success achieved by its own efforts."*   (On Education, p.61)

There lies the core of Russell's approach to children. He wanted them to develop a genuine and deep-seated sense of their own ability to act rightly in the world. He believed, with a measure of good reason, that this was most likely to happen if the child was surrounded by people and things which were available to be seen, touched, smelled, tasted and thought about without unnecessary limitation and conditions.

> *"But while amusements which grown-up people provide should be kept within certain limits, those which the infant can enjoy for itself should be encouraged to the utmost. From the first it should have opportunities to kick and practise its muscles. How our ancestors can have so long persisted in the practice of swaddling-clothes is almost inconceivable; it shows that even parental affection has difficulty in overcoming laziness, since the infant whose limbs are free needs more attention."*   (On Education, p.63)

That observation lies at the root of many others which Russell makes, and which my own experience confirms. Children of any age call for a great deal of careful attention. Russell believed that much of that attention should be given subtly, without too much sentimental dandling and petting, but he was clear that raising a child was a full-time commitment. Despite his strictures against allowing a child to become a tyrant or a parasite, he would not have approved of the way in which most parents and almost all teachers still rank their own convenience far above the intellectual and emotional needs of their children. He was not a de-schooler, but he would not have had much time for our present school system in which the only imperatives are smooth organisation, efficient control and the certainty that if anything goes wrong no adult in the school can be blamed for it. When he ran his own school, Beacon Hill, he tried always to make the getting of knowledge enjoyable. He may not have succeeded with every pupil - even good education sometimes founders on the sheer complexity of its task - but at least he understood that the central issue of all education is not how cost-effective it is, or how efficient it seems to be, but always and only how well it equips the young learner to get on with the rest of his life with his mind intact and still able to function in the new surroundings of adult life.

Russell greatly valued the early part of childhood. He saw that it was a time when a person learns with a unique courage and vivacity. In words which John Holt was to echo in his writings about education, Russell says:

> " ... on the whole an infant's desire to learn is so strong that parents need only provide opportunity. Give the child a chance to develop, and his own efforts will do the rest. It is not necessary to teach a child to crawl, or to walk, or to learn any of the other elements of muscular control. Of course we teach a child to talk by talking to it, but I doubt whether any purpose is served by deliberate attempts to teach words. Children learn at their own pace, and it is a mistake to try to force them."
>
> (On Education, p.65)

It is, perhaps, striking, that a man like Russell, who is remembered for the strength of his commitment to reason, should be able to incorporate into his thinking a point of view which to most people seems irrational and even absurd. I have heard generations of teachers, parents, administrators and politicians confidently assuring each other that children can learn nothing of value unless adults teach it to them. As a teacher myself, I spent most of my professional life convinced that children's thinking was shallow and inconsequential. When I started in the classroom I believed that only by attending my lessons and doing the work I set could a child grow into a cultivated and knowledgeable adult. Unlike Russell, I did not see pre-school learning, even that immensely powerful process by which children acquire their own language (and in some parts of the world two or three others), as anything more than a natural part of the business of getting ready for their encounter with me and my colleagues. We were their real initiators into life.

Since leaving the classroom I have had the leisure, and enough disengagement from the preoccupations of controlling classes of children, to grasp the truth of Russell's argument that children need teaching far less than they need exposure to interesting new knowledge, and the opportunity to interact with it freely. When I was a teacher of French I noticed that 'bright' children often learned lists of nouns, verbs, adjectives and whatnot, but still could not use them to express their own real and important ideas. Indeed, after seven years of enthusiastic study I found myself in France for the first time, having accidentally sent my luggage to the wrong station, unable to have even a simple conversation with a French telephone operator. On the Gare d'Orleans-Austerlitz I sat down and wept, because I spent my adolescence 'learning' something which when put to the test I did not know how to do in any useful way. Yet later, when I worked in French holiday centres for children I routinely met children who had immigrated to France, sometimes only a short time before, but spoke French well enough to pass as natives, and certainly better than me, the one who was shortly to be a teacher. Ironically, they had learned it so well because they needed to be able to speak to potential friends, playmates and people who could give them advantages.

Their knowledge was strictly conditional upon their needing to possess it. If they had been taken from France to some other country, where the language was different, they would certainly have forgotten their French, and learned the local tongue in short order. I knew a doctor who had worked in refugee camps in Thailand. His children, he told me, had quickly learned Thai, and used it in playing and socialising with the local children. Since their return to England, he said, they had forgotten it. As it happened, I taught some of them French in school, and I could testify that, for all their ability to pick up the tonal subtleties of a language as abstruse, to them at least, as Thai, they showed the same resistance to expressing themselves in French as everyone else in their class.

Russell put it most cogently:

> *"It is by what we do ourselves (and for our own reasons, C.R.S) that we learn."*   (On Education, p.65)

Much that we do to our youngest children, for our convenience as often as for cultural and social reasons, was recognised by Russell as potentially dangerous to their happy and harmonious development. He understood how dangerous it is to frighten small children, and how much they need a stable, predictable environment in which the habits they acquire correspond as closely as possible to the 'laws' which govern it. It is perhaps, hard to imagine how little very young children understand about the world, and therefore how imperfectly they are able to fit their actions to its demands. Adults often forget their own childhood experiences, and complacently imagine that their children act from the same elaborate motives as they do. Russell, on the other hand, emphasized the need to reassure children that things will continue to work as they have done in the past.

> *"I have sometimes thought that belief in the uniformity of nature, which is said to be a postulate of science, is entirely derived from the wish for safety. We can cope with the unexpected, but if the laws of nature were suddenly changed, we should perish. The infant, because of its weakness, has need of reassurance, and it will be happier if everything which happens seems to happen according to invariable laws, so as to be predictable."*
> (On Education, p.65)

It is, perhaps, worth remarking that this is both good sense and a strong departure from the norms of our culture. Western Europeans tend to assume that every routine, every repeated activity which we do with our children is aimed at foiling their dangerous, even anarchic drive to break out of the beneficent frameworks which we struggle to erect round them. The truth is, of course, that they want and need routine much more urgently than we adults ever could do.

Russell rejected strongly the whole idea that fear can be used as a tool of education. I have heard teachers, parents and even thoughtful educators suggest that frightening children, and inducing tension in them to keep them focussed on the tasks that make up our adult prescription for their 'education' can be a valuable thing. Indeed, the whole culture of compulsory schooling gives aggressive expression to that idea, and makes a great virtue of forcing young people to do things which give them no pleasure, and very little sense of succeeding in a worthwhile endeavour, simply because, when they grow up 'they will have to do things they don't want to do'.

I feel it is sometimes necessary to call ideas by their proper name, which in this case is 'pure contempt'. Russell saw that frightening children 'for their own good' could never produce mature, self-managing people. Indeed, in the wider context of political life, he was clear in his own mind that the only advantage which could come from raising children with constant fear and incessant reminders that they must do only as they are told in order to be 'good citizens' would be that whenever the 'old men' who governed the country took it into their heads to attack some other nation there would be a ready supply of young men willing to help them do it.

Fear of that kind, deliberately induced in people to make them docile and to kill their capacity for independent thought and action, is common enough in our society. Its influence has spread itself through all parts of the community, to such an extent that even after the uniquely homicidal century the world has just lived through, Governments only have to declare that such-and-such a group of people is 'the Enemy', and most ordinary folk will agree that anyone who tries to understand or negotiate with them is a traitor. Russell, who went to prison during World War 1 for precisely that sort of intellectual independence, lays great stress in all his thinking about education on the simple fact that children who are taught to be cringing, deferential and full of fear will mostly become adults who can be easily deterred from following their own view of the world if it differs from the common one. He wanted children to grow up not anti-social, but confident enough to challenge the package of doctrines, dogmas and idées reçues which their elders try to convince them is the only one worth using.

Russell was not entirely sure where childhood fears originated. He noticed that his children seemed to become more fearful if their nurses, or other adults who looked after them, were themselves timorous. At the same time, he noticed that some of their fears were more instinctive - the reluctance which most humans feel to go into a dark place, or one where they do not feel they can easily predict what will happen. He wanted to eliminate all crippling, irrational terror from children's lives, and keep only the useful kind of fear which alerts a person to real danger.

His approach to his own children seems to have had a lot in common with John Holt's. Holt insisted that parents give themselves many powers and responsibilities which are not theirs by any natural right: the power to punish, for instance, and the power to force their children to make choices in many spheres based not on the child's understanding of life, but only on the adults' idiosyncratic ideas of what is appropriate. There is, however, one essential authority which all parents have and are entitled to wield against their children. It is derived from the simple fact that they have been around longer than their children, and have had a chance to learn what is truly dangerous in their surroundings. Children have not had that chance, and cannot be expected to recognise every danger to their life and health. Parents are always entitled to protect their children, even if those children do not see the reasons for such protective action.

Even so, Russell was reluctant to use irrational fear as tool for keeping children safe. When his son was small he

> " ... lived half the year on a rocky coast where there are many precipices. The boy had no sense whatever of the danger of heights, and would have run straight over a cliff into the sea if we had let him. One day ... we explained to him quietly, as a merely scientific fact, that if he went over the edge he would fall and break like a plate ... He sat still for some time, saying to himself, 'fall, break', and then asked to be taken further from the edge. This was at the age of about two and a half. Since then he has had just enough fear of heights to make him safe while we keep an eye on him. "
> (On Education, pp.71, 72)

Perhaps the reader shares my pleasure on reading about such a gentle, respectful approach to a fellow human being who happens to be at the beginning of his life.

The chief antidote to children's fear is, of course, courage. Many educators, particularly those who work in schools and similar institutions, harbour an unspoken dread of courage in children. They have no problem with youngsters who show the generalised virtues of 'manliness' and 'daring' - the child who performs some feat of sporting brilliance involving determination and self-control, or one who bears a painful illness without too much complaint - but if school pupils decide for themselves to take an independent line of some question of school policy they become on the instant bad, rebellious, dangerous and subject to severe punishment. Critical thought in children is not valued, despite the fact that the aim of all education is to produce adults who, supposedly, can 'think for themselves'.

I remember a boy to whom I taught elementary Latin because he asked me to. He came to me at lunchtime and we spent a little time together exploring the foothills of the language. He was about twelve, intelligent and possessed of an unusual amount of quiet determination. One day, when he came to me for his lesson I noticed that he had been crying. I asked what had happened. He told me that he had decided to leave the school orchestra because he felt that it was not playing serious music, and some of the players were 'goofing off' more often than he felt was right. He had just told the teacher who ran the orchestra of his decision, and she had pressured him, using the arguments that all teachers use in such situations: it was not for him to decide such things, he was letting the others down, and as a mere child he had no right to quit the orchestra without her agreement. He had stood his ground, but the confrontation had taken a lot of emotional energy out of him, and naturally, as a boy of twelve, he had fewer resources than the teacher with which to sustain his self-esteem. Even then, at a time when I was still a cog in the machine of state education, I felt that he was in the right, and told him so. It was not that I did not sympathise with the teacher, who must have felt humiliated by criticism from such an unexpected source, but I also reflected that she was paid to cope with life's little setbacks, and in any case, it was far more important for the boy to develop the courage to stand by his perception of what was right than for authority to win yet another petty battle with a child.

Russell would, I suspect, have broadly agreed with me. He did not think that children should have an exaggerated view of their own importance, but neither did he see great virtue in excessive subordination. Children have their own needs, which may differ from those that adults have, but which should not be crushed underfoot whenever they seem to clash with what grown-ups see as their prerogatives.

Russell also understood, as perhaps many people who take responsibility for children's growth do not, that young people are most likely to develop a strong mental and emotional constitution if they are allowed ample time to play.

> *"Love of play is the most obvious distinguishing mark of young animals, whether human or otherwise. In human children, this is accompanied by an inexhaustible pleasure in pretence. Play and pretence are a vital need of childhood, for*

which opportunity must be provided if the child is to be happy
and healthy, quite independently of any further utility in these
activities."

(On Education, p.81)

I have noticed that deep in our culture of child-rearing is a
suspicion of play. As a race we adults tend to think of play as the
opposite of serious, worthwhile educational activity. Parents and
teachers often say to their children, *"Stop playing now, and get on*
with your homework, chores, tidying-up etc.". Indeed, I remember
once reading in a local newspaper about a school which had
organised a week of recreational activities for their children at a
holiday camp. The children would do some challenging sports and
expeditions, and no doubt have a good time as well. The Education
Committee stepped in and forbade the school to organise the
activity session because it was 'not really educational'! They could
not understand that play and activity are more than a relief from
study: they are the very foundation of healthy intellectual
development.

Russell understood that small children play energetically because
they have a built-in need to model adult behaviour.

"There seems no reason to doubt the most widely accepted
theory, that in play the young of any species rehearse and
practise the activities which they will perform in earnest later
on. The play of puppies is exactly like a dog-fight, except that
they do not actually bite each other. The play of kittens
resembles the behaviour of cats with mice. Children love to
imitate any work they have been watching, such as building
or digging; the more important the work seems to them, the
more they like to play it."

(On Education, p.81)

Play, then, is at one level a desperately serious activity, aimed at
helping children to initiate themselves into the life they already
realise they will have to live in earnest at some time in the
unfathomable future. In Russell's view, children perceive
adulthood as primarily about having and wielding power.

"Some psycho-analysts have tried to see a sexual symbolism
in children's play. This, I am convinced, is utter moonshine.
The main instinctive urge of childhood is not sex, but the

> *desire to become adult, or, perhaps more correctly, the will*
> *to power."* (On Education, p.82)

Experience leads me to think that he is right, and that adults often overbear and trivialise their children's play precisely because they dimly realise that the youngsters are struggling to rise above the inferiority they perceive in themselves and attain as quickly as possible the position of power and influence they know that the adults around them have reached. I often hear adults justifying their repression of children with the argument that 'they mustn't be allowed to get above themselves', or that ' they need to know that they are not grown-ups yet'.

Russell understood that children are not in any danger of misunderstanding their status:

> *"The child is impressed with his own weakness in*
> *comparison with older people, and he wishes to become their*
> *equal. I remember my boy's profound delight when he*
> *realised that he would one day be a man and that I had once*
> *been a child; one could see effort being stimulated by the*
> *realisation that success was possible."* (On Education, p.82)

Looked at in that perspective, play can be recognised as an essential means by which a child engages with the challenge of maturity. By thwarting the impulse to play, as we do so often in the West, because we believe it diverts the children's attention from much more important enterprises, we actually retard the growth of adult-like behaviours.

> *"From a very early age, the child wishes to do what older*
> *people do, as is shown by the practice of imitation. Older*
> *brothers and sisters are useful, because their purposes can be*
> *understood and their capacities are not so far out of reach as*
> *those of grown-up people. The feeling of inferiority is very*
> *strong in children; when they are normal and rightly*
> *educated, it is a stimulus to effort, but if they are repressed it*
> *may become a source of unhappiness."* (On Education, p.82)

Simply stated, the view of play which emerges from Russell's writing is that it is the child's work. It harnesses the will to power, and allows the child to explore it and discover which uses of it are acceptable, sociable, likely to lead to innocent gratification, and which are dangerous both to the individual and society. It may be surmised that much of the aggression and egoism which is often found in growing children is the bitter fruit not of insufficient education, but rather the all-encompassing adult control of what happens to children. By denying children expression, teachers and parents prevent their discovery of life in all its variety, and block the development of skills which are really valuable throughout life.

"Education consists in the cultivation of instincts, not in their suppression. Human instincts are very vague, and can be satisfied in a great variety of way. Most of them require, for their gratification, some kind of skill. Cricket and baseball satisfy the same instinct, but the boy will play whichever he has learnt. Thus the secret of instruction, in so far as it bears upon character, is to give a man such kinds of skill as shall lead to his employing his instincts usefully. The instinct of power, which in the child is crudely satisfied by identification with Bluebeard (or some other storybook image of tyranny and merciless strength), can find in later life a refined satisfaction by scientific discovery, or artistic creation, or the creation and education of splendid children, or any one of a thousand useful activities."   (On Education, p.8)

Russell recognised that in our Western culture, instinct is commonly understood to be dangerous. He was convinced that:

"Neither the old belief in original sin, nor Rousseau's belief in natural virtue, is in accordance with the facts. The raw material of instinct is ethically neutral, and can be shaped either to good or evil by the influence of the environment."
(On Education, p.90)

Inevitably, this line of thought led him to reflect on the virtues and vices of the education he saw going on around him. He knew best the education of upper-class children, and noted that many of them grew up with their minds controlled by the most destructive thoughts. In the ordinary English upper-class family:

" ... the killing of birds is considered highly creditable, and the killing of men in war is regarded as the noblest of professions."   (On Education, p.92)

It is tempting to pass over this aspect of Russell's thinking about education without paying any further attention to it. Nowadays we do not generally encourage children to hunt and shoot, and the abolition of national service has made killing the Queen's enemies something one can choose to do or not do. Nonetheless, I think Russell's observations about the influence environment wields over children are still valid. Schools try harder now than they did in former times to be 'welcoming'. They usually have flowers in the entrance and multi-lingual notices conveying the message that they are happy to have people coming into them. Yet when children go into them they are still surrounded with the strong imperatives of imposed power. Schools are not places where children explore their own potential. They are places where they are subject to instruction which they cannot escape, and tested competitively to see how well they have absorbed that instruction. This teaches them the subtle but enduring belief that people have different value according to their ability to perform certain tasks set by a faceless and anonymous external authority. The inescapable result of that process is that many children leave school and turn into adults who despise themselves, and undervalue their real abilities.

Russell comments on this aspect of education from the standpoint of one who acquired a high culture by his own efforts and for his own reasons.

> *"Even in purely intellectual matters it is possible to have a constructive or a destructive bias. A classical education is almost entirely critical: a boy learns to avoid mistakes, and to despise those who commit them. This tends to produce a kind of cold correctness, in which originality is replaced by respect for authority."*   (On Education, p.94)

It is precisely that precision which politicians are incessantly seeking to introduce into more and more areas of school life. Russell felt that children did not benefit from it, because their minds are much more experimental and constructive than adults'.

> *"Wherever avoidance of error is the chief thing aimed at, education tends to produce an intellectually bloodless type. The prospect of doing something venturesome with one's knowledge ought to be held before all the abler young men and young women."*   (On Education, p.94)

I suspect that the reader will want, as I do, to include every young person, whether 'abler' or not, in that prescription!

Chapter three

Russell and schooling

Bertrand Russell never fails to surprise his readers. Writing as a product of home-centred schooling one might expect him to approve of it with few reservations. He lived, however, at a time when many working-class children lived in surroundings almost unimaginably squalid and cramped. What would be counted poverty today might have seemed not far removed from luxury to children brought up in the tenements which were all that many wage-earners could afford. Russell assumed that most youngsters could not be successfully educated at home, if only because children need space in which to develop. He also recognised that working-class life was often blighted by the stress and anxiety imposed on adults by the grinding imbalance between the physical demands which their daily lives and work forced them to endure, and the pitifully low wages on which they had to live.

Therefore, he felt that, in an imperfect world, boarding schools were probably the best places to educate children. Many would probably disagree with him, or stipulate that only a place like Summerhill could meet the children's real needs. In fact, Russell knew about Summerhill, and thought enough of it to use his influence to help Neill when the authorities would not let him employ a Frenchman to teach French. Perhaps he was thinking of an institution not unlike Summerhill when he suggested that children's needs could be met most successfully at a boarding school.

The chief advantage of boarding schools, in Russell's opinion, was that they could be,

> " ... *in the country in the best surroundings, whereas day schools, for most children, must be in the town. Another argument, which applies in many cases though not in all, is that home is likely to be a place where a child is subjected to nervous strain. It may be that the parents quarrel, that the*

mother is over-anxious, that the father is unkind."
(Education and the Social Order, p.45)

It is tempting to see this view of schooling as simplistic. The home-schooling movement of the latter part of the 20th Century would certainly object to Russell's overarching assumption that working-class families are not generally the best environment for children to receive their education. In his defence, however, I would stress that he was writing about a time before social insurance, the National Health, television and computers, and the working-class life he observed was still, in many cases 'nasty, brutish and short'. Ironically, for all the social progress we have seen in the last fifty years, I remember only about fifteen years ago asking the Deputy Head of an urban school where I was teaching if he could think of anything in his school, apart from the toilets and the lunches, which happened because a child expressed a need for it. He paused for a long moment, and then said *"Well, the school is a better place for many of them than their own homes"*. The point was certainly a good one - many of his pupils came from loveless and strife-filled homes - but the fact that he could not point to any intellectual need of theirs that his school was meeting was disturbing, to say the least. Russell, on the other hand, would have been able to talk about the children's mental and emotional development in school, because he passionately rejected the idea of traditional imposed study. Boarding schools appealed to him mainly because in them it might be possible to provide the variety of stimuli and social groupings which children needed if they were to discover and develop their own potentialities.

Russell and 'The Herd'

Russell writes with an uncommon measure of detachment about the influence which their peers exert upon children. He does not himself seem to have been part of any large group of children during his own childhood, and he is well-known for having stood apart from the main stream of political and social thought when he became an adult. Nonetheless, his books on education show that he understood as well as any other educationist, and better than many who try to run the lives of children, that the community of young people among whom any person grows up has the power to distort or even destroy in that person essential mental and emotional mechanisms. He understood that children learn from the 'herd' many of the lessons which determine their character as adults.

Indeed, he believed that the habits and ways of thinking which people learn from their peers are often the ones which mark their adult lives most deeply, and are hardest to eradicate if they happen to be bad.

The 'herd' can, of course, be a safe, protective environment for a certain type of child. The conformist, the boy or girl who goes through life asking only what they need to do in order to be safe, will often emerge from their schooling quite convinced that it is always right to do what the others are doing, never asking whether that pattern of behaviour is humane, just or even moral. The group sanctifies and justifies whatever it has collectively set out to do, and if asked why they are acting as they, are its members see no need for any reply beyond: *"Everyone was doing it"*. Russell, however, had watched with growing concern the ease with which large groups of people, both children and adults, could be persuaded to do unconscionable things, including persecuting other races and going to war. He had met the original of George Arthur, the saintly schoolboy in *Tom Brown's Schooldays* - his cousin, Dean Stanley - and it is easy to imagine him reading that novel with a particular interest in the character of the boy who, though jeered at and ill-treated for holding to a moral code so much higher than that of his contemporaries, stands his ground and in the end compels his fellows to share it.

> *"For certain exceptionally strong characters, there is an educational value in standing out against the herd for some reason profoundly felt to be important. Such action strengthens the will, and teaches a man self-reliance. Provided he is not made to suffer too much, this may be all for the good; but if the herd makes him unhappy beyond a point, he will either yield and lose what was most excellent in his character, or become filled with destructive rage, which may, as in Napoleon's case, (not to mention Hitler's - C.R.S.) do untold harm to the world. "*
> (Education and the Social Order, p.62)

In short, Russell did not see the unmitigated influence of the herd as a valuable element in education. When it operates legitimately, consciously balancing the individual's need to act independently and the right of the community to preserve the structures by means of which it pursues its reasonable common goals, he was happy with it. But as he realised, through the experience of a long and varied life, it is hard to guarantee that the herd will always use its power beneficently. Certainly, experience shows that in many - too many - places where young people are prepared for adult life, the peer group holds absolute sway over the lives of almost all of them. It amazes me that in England, a supposedly advanced country, a steady stream of schoolchildren kill themselves because going to school has become for them so unbearably awful that even death seems more inviting. In most cases, these young people destroy themselves because other children have decided to persecute them, not just for a few hours, or even days, but endlessly, concentrating on them the anger, frustration, bitterness and unfocussed rage that powerless people commonly feel, and cannot express in any other way. Yet for some reason, no-one closes down the places where these things happen until the adults who run them can guarantee that being a pupil there will not lead to death or madness. Instead, these frightful acts of oppression warrant little more than a report in the press, a few police interviews and a special assembly to remember the departed.

It is clear, then, that the herd has become a strong element in the whole experience which is school-based education, without ever having been examined, understood, and properly controlled. It influences the lives of many of them more directly and powerfully than all the teaching, testing and rulemaking that adults assume the school is supposed to do for their notional benefit. It crushes in many pupils any sense they might have had that study and skill are worth at least as much as pop music, fashion or just being one of the 'in' crowd. It confers great, and arbitrary, power on people who have not yet developed the ability to use it for the good of all. The youngster who is popular, often precisely because he refuses to conform even with reasonable rules, can easily become the arbiter of what is acceptable behaviour amongst his peers. If he seems to be able to break petty and irrational rules, which exist in many schools for the convenience of the Staff, and endure the consequences, his fellows will not generally ask themselves whether his behaviour has any enduring value, to himself or to them. They will simply follow him and join in his escapades because they make him seem glamorous. They will want to share in his prestige by collaborating with him and imitating his behaviour. The herd will follow him because that is what herds do. The school may in the end solve the problem he poses to its smooth running by expelling him, but the teachers who manage it are unlikely to ask the only question really worth asking about him, which is: how can an institution which is supposed to be supremely beneficial to children allow its community life to develop in such a way that some the most influential people in it are the ones who attack everything it exists to do?

Russell wrote:

> *"The man who wishes to found a good school must think more about the character of the herd which he is creating than about any other single element. If he himself is kindly and tolerant, but permits the school herd to be cruel and intolerant, the boys under his care will experience a painful environment in spite of his excellence."*
>
> (Education and the Social Order, p.60)

He recognised that even in progressive schools bullying and philistinism are a constant danger, particularly if the school is run in a non-interventionist way, like some early experimental schools. He also saw, however, danger in the traditional heavy-handed way in which adults have always tried to regulate children's behaviour. No doubt Dean Stanley pointed out to him that even during Thomas Arnold's relatively enlightened reign over Rugby School the prospect of receiving a flogging with the birch rod, a punishment which we would nowadays call 'torture', did not deter either the original of Harry Flashman and his fellow bullies, or the likes of Tom Brown from breaking school rules. As he writes in 'Education and the Social Order':

> *"If the grown-ups exercise force in their dealings with the older children, the older children will, in their turn, exercise force in their dealings with the smaller ones."*   (p.61)

In fact, he understood, as Professor Roland Meighan once observed to me, that a school is usually a 'bully environment' in itself, unless strong and clear-sighted steps have been taken to spread the regulatory power of the community widely among its members by allowing all of them to take part in controlling and directing it, so that they no longer see themselves as powerless helots who constantly look for subversive ways to run at least a small part of their lives.

Russell saw clearly that an unregulated 'herd' tended to create timid, lacklustre people, who took pains to avoid any kind of unconventional behaviour, even when such behaviour might be the only just, humane or moral course of action available to them. Courage and force of character, the determination to do right even when the whole society in which one lives has decided to do wrong, are surely worth striving to produce in every generation of young people. Only by creating masses of people who have enough self-possession to say 'no' to national leaders who want to lead their nations to war can we hope to have lasting peace. Russell, in his own generation, went to prison because the 'herd' of his time had collectively accepted the decision of their Government to go to war, while he had decided for himself that no Government had the right to force unwilling people to sacrifice their private beliefs, their health and even their lives to a piece of nationalistic folly, a war without justification between armies of people who had absolutely no reason to hate, and still less kill each other.

Unfortunately, the 'herds' which engulf and strongly influence young people are rarely sensitive and courageous. They do not often encourage dissent. Indeed, schools cannot tolerate much critical self-determination in their pupils because their authority can only operate effectively when it is more or less seamless. Russell himself would probably have been a difficult pupil if he had attended school during his childhood and early adolescent years, since it is hard to imagine him doing anything simply because 'it's the rule'. He would certainly have wanted to know how the rule came to be made, and what reasonable concerns it was supposed to meet. He would have had no compunction about refusing to obey, just as he did in later years when he embarrassed the Government in the 1960s by his resistance to the morally untenable idea that any civilised country could use nuclear weapons against another nation.

Russell's fundamental mind-set made him conscious of the dilemma which faces all parents when they set about preparing their children for life in a world which is real, not by any means perfect, and likely to impinge upon them in ways which are complex and unforeseeable.

> *"With regard to the larger herd that lies outside the school, parents whose opinions are in any way unconventional are faced with a perplexity which many of them find very difficult to resolve. If they send their children to a school where*

unusual opinions are encouraged, or where unusual freedoms are permitted, they fear that, on entering the larger world, the boys or girls will not be readily adaptable to things as they are. Those who have been allowed to think and speak about sex will be oppressed by the usual reticences and pruderies. Those who have not been taught about patriotism will have a difficulty in finding a niche in our nationalistic world. ... And, in a word, those who have been used to freedom will find the chains of slavery more irksome than those who have been slaves from birth. Such, at least, is the argument which I have frequently heard advanced by liberal-minded parents in favour of an illiberal education for their children. "   (Education and the Social Order, p.63)

Russell and the curriculum

A parent once asked me, during a question-period after a talk I had given, whether there was any traditional school subject which I considered essential, and which I would require children to study, whether they wanted to or not. I thought carefully before replying, because although I was clear in my own mind that my answer was 'no', I had never been asked this particular question before, and I wasn't sure whether I could defend my stance convincingly. When I gave my answer there was an entirely understandable indrawing of breath, and some hostile questioning. I realised that we British have still a long way to go before we feel really safe with a curriculum which is a catalogue and not a prescription. Russell would not have agreed with me, if I understand his writing on this aspect of education rightly. He accepted that not every young person needed to learn every aspect of human knowledge, but he had undergone enough traditional teaching, albeit delivered by tutors rather than class teachers, to have absorbed the idea that all children need at least a smattering of the learning which we still think of as 'basic' or 'the core subjects' - maths, English, geography, history and so forth, the subjects which we treat as 'essential' because we have teachers for them who need to be employed.

Russell, however, would have agreed with many other serious educators of more modern times that the grim-faced, repetitive, lacklustre rote-learning so common in the early days of state schooling, and the heavy handed, competitive driving of knowledge into young minds which is still promoted by the government through its League Table and ceaseless testing was an offence against the very soul of our youth, and should be eliminated at all costs. He insisted that the presentation of knowledge to young people needed to be attractive and intriguing. About geography he wrote,

> *"Almost every child becomes interested in geography as soon as it is associated with the idea of travel. I should teach geography partly by pictures and tales about travellers, but mainly by the cinema, showing what the traveller sees on his journey. The knowledge of geographical facts is useful, **but without intrinsic intellectual value** (emphasis mine, CRS); when, however, geography is made vivid by pictures, it has the merit of giving food for imagination."*
>
> (On Education, p.171)

I do not read into this any sense that somehow a child's intellectual life would be permanently harmed if he or she did not know the set list of facts which constitute 'school geography'. Rather, it seems as if Russell, himself more or less a polymath, believed that every person, given the right opportunities and teaching methods, could develop a lively interest in geography, and by the same token, in any other subject. Only the circumstances in which it is taught: the method adopted by the teacher, the amount of new learning the child has to do during each lesson, and the relevance of its presentation influence the learner's response. The idea is seductive: if we could only remove the obstacles to learning which schools routinely create, and even treat as positive virtues, we could raise a generation of clear-sighted adults, armed with a wide knowledge of the world and confident of their ability to add to it, whenever it becomes necessary to do so.

At this point I ask the reader to forgive me for talking about my own education. To a large extent, Russell's thoughts about 'essential' school subjects speak vividly to me as I remember my own schooling. Like me, Russell was, by his own admission, not very good at arithmetic. He wept, as I did, over the multiplication table. I imagine that his tutors would not have thought of him as a future mathematician of the first rank. He went on to overcome his early problems, and to realise that mathematics is almost infinitely more interesting that mere calculation. He managed to discover the intrinsic beauty and challenge of mathematics because he had the freedom, at some stage, to examine its structure, to uncover the beautiful network of universal linkages which enables us to see how the elements of our universe are knit together. He also went on to understand how that knowledge could be used.

I, on the other hand, did not. Like every other five-year-old, I encountered numbers as a set of signs which I began dimly to understand were related to groups of objects. No-one had the wit to see that if they wanted me to do sums I needed to have some concrete purpose for that activity. Just telling me to write numbers down on paper, and then do mechanical procedures like adding or dividing brought me no intellectual satisfaction at all, only a sense that this was something I had to do, like going to school or having injections, because I was what I was - a child. When I wept, as I did, over pages of calculations, it was not because I was intellectually frustrated. It was simply because the sheer mechanical effort of juggling numbers, not fully understanding why I was doing it, threw a shadow over everything else I did at school and at home. However well I was able to read and talk, I could not do these wretched sums. In the strange, brilliant but confusing world I found myself in, there was something which all the big, powerful people around me thought was very important, but which I could not make head nor tail of. It is hard to appreciate how hurtful this can be for a small child. Most of us went through an experience like this with some part of the curriculum, but we are, perhaps, so grateful for having emerged from childhood that we are careful not to hoard any bad memories of it, lest they make us too indulgent with our own children, or too 'soft' in our reaction to their difficulties.

Russell, who remembered 'weeping bitterly' because he could not learn the multiplication table, would, I imagine have recognised the importance of not overloading children with enforced learning at a time when they are most open to false beliefs about themselves based on their limited ability to absorb new knowledge. He always made a strong case for linking learning to pleasurable and gratifying experiences.

In his comments on the learning of English literature he emphasised the value of learning by heart the best parts of our heritage of creative language. We have, perhaps, lost our taste for knowing things well enough to be able to recite them from memory. We can easily recall information from databases, without even the inconvenience of looking it up in books. We tend to see memorisation as 'rote-learning', and less valuable to youngsters than being able to find information from established sources when and where it is needed. There is a lot to be said for our adaptation to an information-rich environment, but to lose entirely the mechanisms by which we furnish our minds with permanent resources in the form of memorable ideas and beautiful words would be a sad loss of intellectual independence. With Russell, we can rightly militate for education in which the sheer joy of learning fine words leads to the deep pleasure of using them in plays and recitation to express our own deepest feelings.

> *"I remember (he wrote) the exquisite amusement with which I acted the quarrel scene between Brutus and Cassius, and declaimed:*
>> *'I had rather be a dog and bay the moon,*
>> *Than such a Roman'*
> *Children who take part in performing* Julius Caesar *or* The Merchant of Venice, *any other suitable play, will not only know their own parts, but most of the other parts as well. The play will be in their thoughts for a long time, and all by way of enjoyment."*   (On Education, p.175)

Russell was convinced that the difficulty and 'adultness' of the greatest works of literature were not the main reasons why children did not commonly master them at school. He was caustic about the type of literature which schools often served up to their pupils because it was written for them as children, drained of real depth and emotional complexity. Having seen small children being dragged kicking and screaming through the 'Adventures of (say) Roderick the Red Pirate', I can testify that books written for youngsters who are perceived as having a low 'reading age' are constructed not to fulfil the imperatives of a good strong story, vivid language and challenging plot, but simply to ensure that the reader encounters the words which are deemed to be within his or her grasp. In these books the story, if there is one, is often facile. It may well have no point of contact with the child's real life-experience. Indeed, I well remember the furore which broke out in the late 60s when a children's author, Leila Berg, wrote some books for young readers in which the characters were poor, lived in run-down Council flats, and spoke more or less like the children who read about them. Most commentators dwelt on the 'lowering of standards' implicit in the author's free use of the vivid jargon of working-class kids. They complained that they were trying to eliminate this way of speaking, discouraging children from using it in class, and, by implication, classifying everyone for whom it was a natural idiom as intellectually as well as socially inferior. They seemed not to have noticed that they had been failing in this purpose since the beginning of compulsory schooling. Generations of working-class kids had emerged from their education still using their London dialect, and untouched by the higher culture their teachers had laboured to impart to them.

Russell wrote:

> " ... *good literature is intended to give pleasure, and if children cannot be got to derive pleasure from it they are hardly likely to derive benefit either.*" (On Education, p.175)

He saw that subjecting children to literature as if it were nasty medicine could only kill their interest at its source. The teachers who rejected books set in warm, scatty but positive working class families because, though they were engaging and full of interest, they did not come from the middle-class canon of 'proper writing', did not convert many of their young pupils into devotees of our literary heritage. They only convinced them that this kind of writing was not, and could never be, for them.

Russell's strongest condemnation was levelled at a strain of writing for children which did not take account of their essential seriousness.

> *"Sentimentality, in dealing with children and elsewhere, is a failure of dramatic sympathy. No child thinks it charming to be childish; he wants, as soon as possible, to learn to behave like a grown-up person. Therefore, a book for children ought never to display a patronising pleasure in childish ways"*
> (On Education, p.175)

We should, perhaps, compare this robust declaration with the insistence, so often heard in discussions between adults about child-rearing, that 'children must be given the right to be children' or that 'we must preserve children's innocence'. 'Innocence' sounds like a virtue, but when applied to children it means an artificial retardation of their emotional and intellectual growth. 'Innocent' children do not have opinions because they are not allowed to acquire knowledge which might be inconvenient for adults to confront and to live with. 'Innocent' children can be told 'white' lies - and even the other kind - if adults think it is necessary in order to keep them in a different category of being. In short, 'innocent' children are no threat to adults, and to their often precarious control of their surroundings. Russell stood with some of the most radical educational thinkers, such as John Holt and A.S. Neill in believing that children can handle any kind of information if it is presented in an accessible way, and if adults are prepared to answer their questions about it honestly. I suspect that if this principle were more commonly applied in educating children there would be less reason for parents and teachers to worry about their children's eyes falling on such adult literature as the pornographic magazines and erotic books so often displayed on the upper shelves of newsagents and bookshops. Children who have not been sensitised to the mingled sense of daring and excitement which surrounds this kind of literature can see how silly it is, and how limited is the pleasure that can be derived from it, compared with truly great writing and pictorial art.

Modern languages also figured in Russell's curriculum. He recognised, as generations of teachers have, before his time and since, that language-teaching is always going to be a problem. English children do not often master foreign languages at school. As a language teacher myself, I have often taken over classes who had studied French for any up to four years, only to find the students unable to understand the simplest ideas, or to express any thought beyond the five or six conventional phrases with which most language-teaching begins. These were not the pupils of idle or inefficient teachers. They had often been taught by the most senior teacher in the language department. I once took over a group of youngsters who had been taught French by a young man of exceptional charisma and skill, only to discover that the advanced language skills they had seemed to possess when he was teaching them had evaporated when they came under the influence of a mere journeyman such as me. The fact is that children will not learn another language than their own unless we provide them with a powerful incentive. Continental children, particularly the Dutch and Scandinavians, learn to speak good English at an early age. I suspect that this happens because the truly important things in their young lives - pop music, fashion, films, American culture and sport - are mediated to them predominantly through English.

English children have no such powerful motive for learning, say, French or German.

Russell believed that modern languages could and should be taught to young people at the earliest age possible. He also felt that they were best taught by people whose native tongue they were. This is undoubtedly an essential prerequisite for real language-learning. I always felt that it was somewhat absurd for me to utter streams of French, even in an accent which, though not perfect, has enabled me to pass as a Frenchman for a short time at least, when everyone in the classroom knew that I could say the same thing with a far greater chance of being understood, in English. If I had done what the situation cried out for me to do - refuse to speak English at all, and hope that they would pick up my meaning by some sort of induction - I should, no doubt, have succumbed to classroom chaos in very short order.

Russell, speaking from the standpoint of one who had been educated largely by tutors, suggested that children might best learn another language if it were presented to them at a very early age by people who had some caring rôle to play in their lives, such as nurses or 'nannies'. He was right, I think, because language is supremely a mode of communication. Small children desperately want to communicate with the world around them, and if from time to time that world happens to use a different set of sounds from their parents, they learn it, and use it appropriately. It may take them a little time to master all the nuances of the new tongue, but they have not yet learned - from schooling - that it is more important to avoid mistakes than it is to say something useful in it. Therefore, they soon find themselves joining in an easy rapport with whoever speaks the language with them. Their natural faculty for exploring the wonders of the world around them, married to their complete absence of self-consciousness, allows very small children quickly to become effective second-language speakers. Russell understood this clearly when he wrote:

> *"I think, therefore, that every school for children should have a French mistress, and if possible a German mistress too, who should not formally instruct the children in her language, except quite at first, but should play games with them, and talk to them, and make the success of the games depend on their understanding and answering. She could start with* Frère Jacques *and* Sur le Pont d'Avignon, *and go*

> *on gradually to more complicated games. In this way the language could be acquired without any mental fatigue, and with all the pleasure of play-acting."*
> (On Education, pp.176-7)

This understanding of language-learning corresponds closely to the ideas which emerge every few years from reports and pilot-studies initiated by the Government in response to the feeling that, as one of the more prominent members of the European Union, Britain should be producing substantially more good speakers of European languages than it does at present. Language-teachers have seen them come and go, but little has changed in the nation's schools, simply because you cannot teach language effectively to groups of thirty more or less unwilling learners unless you happen to possess a rare combination of insight and charisma. Most of us do not, and the result is generations of children who, like many I have met, leave school with a G.C.S.E. pass in French or German, but cannot say the simplest things in the countries where those languages are spoken. Successful language-learning needs a certain measure of immersion and sustained exposure to the sounds and cadences of the target language. Anything less than that is a waste of time.

Chapter four

Religion, class and patriotism in education

Religion

Religion and education have always run together as if they were the most intimate of fellows. Russell, as most readers will know, did not number religion among his interests, and saw it as an obstacle to unfettered thought and good science. I, as it happens, am a Christian of the evangelical variety. I sympathise, however, with Russell's approach to religion because I have seen beliefs like mine fathered upon generations of school-children by means which Jesus himself would have repudiated, under the colour of 'Religious Education'. As a Christian, I want to see others making 'spiritual' choices, if they make them at all, for authentic, personal reasons, not because someone whose opinion they have been told they must trust leaves them no choice to make between accepting or rejecting that person's teaching.

Russell was magnanimous towards religion, because he regarded it as a social phenomenon, with its own unique set of merits and dangers.

> " ... although the moral codes resulting from religion have been curious, it must be admitted that it is religion that has given rise to them. If any morality is better than none, then religion has been a force for good."
>
> (Education and the Social Order, p.66)

In his day, most of the more prestigious schools, particularly the Public Schools, had some connection with the Churches which proclaimed one or other of the long-established forms of Christianity. In formulating his ideas about the place of religion in education he acknowledged that the social 'colour' of the nation was likely to be affected by religious teaching for a long time to come. He insisted, however, that its influence needed to be examined and questioned because in the form in which it was propagated in schools it had a number of specific bad effects on the minds of young learners.

His first concern about religion was that it expected people to take doctrinal statements on faith, and not to assess their rationality:

" ... *any exceptionally intelligent child, who discovers by reflection that the arguments for immortality are inconclusive, will be discouraged by his teachers, perhaps even punished; and other children who show any inclination to think likewise will be discouraged from conversation On such topics, and if possible prevented from reading books that might increase their knowledge and their reasoning power."* (Education and the Social Order, p.69)

We should, perhaps, reflect that children do, naturally, adopt the ideas which their teachers propose to them for no stronger reason than that those ideas come from the same person who determines what they shall learn of ordinary, 'secular' subjects, and whom they assume to be trustworthy because they are also certainly knowledgeable. Many youngsters never throw off their trust in the word of people they have always known as confident, unchallengeable, and full of certainty based on apparently deep and accurate study. That religion is not in the same category as, say, biology or mathematics, because its propositions cannot be verified objectively, ought to be clearly understood by anyone who intends to study it. Yet it is frequently taught, particularly in Church Schools, as if it were a catalogue of truths on a par with the best of contemporary scientific knowledge. Indeed, since the beginning of organised universal schooling in this country it has remained the only compulsory subject.

Russell would have it otherwise. He has harsh words to say about teachers who consent to work in schools where religion is a strong influence on daily life:

" ... *since most people whose intelligence is much above the average are nowadays openly or secretly agnostic, the teachers in a school which insists upon religion must be either stupid or hypocritical, unless they belong to that small class of men who, owing to some kink, have intellectual ability without intellectual judgement."*

(Education and the Social Order, p.69)

He did not, perhaps, foresee that later generations of schoolteachers would have to respond to the influx of children from many other cultures and traditions. This has introduced into traditional religious instruction a healthy measure of the sort of study which more up-to-date schools are calling 'Comparative Religion'. It treats religion as a social phenomenon and claims to prepare children to live in a multi-cultural civilisation in which many different modes of worship and ways of living coexist, by exposing them to the doctrines and practices of those religions and trying to show that those who believe them are all sincere and convinced that they are doing right. The problem this shift of emphasis poses to educators is that, for all its apparent objectivity, Comparative Religion is still forced upon pupils by an establishment which holds that religion is a sort of vaccination agent against bad behaviour and inconvenient thought, and therefore it will always be presented, more or less unsubtly, as something which children 'need' to know about in order for them to become good citizens. If it were an optional course of study there would be little to complain of. As the only compulsory subject in the old curriculum, however, it is still sanctified in the national mind as one of the prime means by which we tame our children's unruly spirits and compel them to live by standards which, incidentally, we would never dream of applying to ourselves.

Russell saw the influence of religion as essentially conservative. Opinions which have a religious basis are extremely difficult to modify or abandon, even if good sense and common humanity suggest that they are wrong in the context of modern life. As Russell pointed out:

> " ... in our own day men do things from religious motives which, apart from religion, would seem intolerably cruel. The Roman Catholic Church still believes in hell. The Anglican Church, as a result of a decision of the lay members of the Privy Council against the opposition of the Archbishops of Canterbury and York, does not regard hell as de fide: nevertheless, most Anglican clergymen still believe in hell. All who believe in hell must regard vindictive punishment as permissible, and therefore have a theoretical justification for cruel methods in education and the treatment of criminals."

(Education and the Social Order, p.71)

I have often noticed how easily genuinely loving Christian people, who live in harmony with their families and their community, leap to the defence of those who take illiberal positions and advocate the harsh treatment of people who fall below what they think of as high moral standards. I have met a good few believers in the teachings of Jesus who insist that God wants murderers to be hanged, children to be beaten regularly, homosexuals punished and even, sometimes - though I blush to tell of it - heretics to be put in prison. They tend to insist that England is a 'Christian country' and therefore that Christianity should have a privileged position within it. What that means in practical terms is generally that any part of the Bible which seems to underpin 'old-fashioned', harsh attitudes to others should be applied with the utmost rigour. I find myself, even as an evangelical Christian, siding with Russell against such notions. I choose to be bound by Christian principles because, when you strip off all the reactionary primitivism which tends to adhere to writing which had its origins in the desert and the feudal kingdoms of the middle east, what remains is sublime. The Christian message is grounded in an unconditional love of mankind. It teaches that every other human being is the believer's 'neighbour', to whom he or she is totally obligated, in spite of all the differences and hatreds which have grown up because it is always much easier to hate than to love, and to reject without examination others' customs and habits.

Russell and Social Class in education

There is a small but tangible pleasure to be gained from reading what Russell had to say about the question of class in education. As a minor aristocrat himself, it is easy to imagine him seeing the greatest possible virtue in having a society led by those whose undaunted sense of their own natural superiority enabled them to set standards for everyone else, and benevolently, but firmly, insist on having those standards adhered to by everybody who wanted to be thought of a good citizens. He recognised that the English class system was deeply entrenched, partly because it derived from a social structure grounded in ancient conquests, and in the possession of land and wealth through the happenstance of inheritance. This had led to the emergence of a truly bizarre belief that the 'best' kind of education was that which had little or nothing to do with physical work. 'Gentlemen' needed to know a modicum of the Classics, in the original languages, but nothing about gardening or carpentry. It mattered little if they did not remember much of what they had learned in their Public Schools, since few of them would ever use it in life. I am reminded of the fiasco which occurred during the Boer War, when the officers of the Army, casting around for some code or cipher which they could use to pass secret messages, decided to use Latin, since they had all studied it under compulsion at such places as Eton and Harrow. The scheme did not work, they discovered, because hardly any of them actually knew enough of the language to communicate even the simplest ideas. They had done the work, struggled through their daily construe with the help of cribs and dictionaries, but had not actually retained more than the smallest smattering of knowledge in their heads.

Russell saw that this concentration on more or less abstract, academic knowledge was a serious drag on progress. He expressed his feelings on the subject with a certain whimsy:

> "A gentleman is intended to be ornamental rather than useful, but in order to be adequately ornamental he has to be supplied with an unearned income. For those who have to earn their living, it is hardly wise to attempt a form of education whose main purpose was to make idleness elegant. There is no such thing nowadays as an all-round education, but there is a tendency, especially in England, to over-emphasise those elements in education which enable a man to talk with seeming intelligence."
>
> (Education and the Social Order, p.98)

He realised that education had become a class issue, from the very first days of universal compulsory schooling, because it had become an instrument for directing people into the kind of study which would best fit them for the line of work which the governing class had decided was good for them. This way of working with young people was relatively easy to justify in the days when our economy was built upon labour-intensive factory work, heavy industry and mining. No-one then questioned the assumption that the greater part of the male population would have to accept more or less menial work done for low wages in conditions characterised by a stultifying concentration on 'getting the job done', not questioning work-conditions, and accepting that the employer's needs took precedence even over the stability and happiness of the worker's family.

The revolution in electronics and information technology - and it is truly a revolution - has altered the life of the rising generation more radically than any other technical advance since steam was harnessed two centuries ago. It could even be argued that modern cybernetic technology has changed man's potential for progress as much as the wheel. It has put within the grasp of every person the means to realise his or her wildest dreams. The Internet, by enabling anyone who has a computer to bring into his home information of any kind, at any time of the day or night, allows even the youngest children, if they wish it, to learn complex skills and to develop their own array of abilities and interests. Because it is interesting and exciting to use, children routinely master the computer. They often manage to do things with it which their parents would have expected only grown-ups - and mainly intense, bespectacled, white-coated, graduate grown-ups - to be capable of.

Russell's strictures about the influence of class on what is taught in schools would, I suspect, have provided him with the grounds for a particularly pointed argument against our present National Curriculum, if only he had lived a few years longer. He would have criticised its conservatism, and its failure to incorporate the powerful liberating influence of digital technology. He would certainly have pointed out that, in contrast to the stratified model of society which schools served in his day, modern education needs desperately to throw off the assumptions on which it has always based its content.

In his day, schools prepared their pupils either for life as leaders, rulers, and exemplars of culture, or as cogs in the vast mechanism of an industrial society, possessed of no more knowledge than their rulers thought good for them to have, most of it purely utilitarian in nature. The majority were expected to have enough literacy and numeracy to be able to understand and account for the transactions they would have to carry out in creating wealth for their masters. Beyond that, they needed nothing from the treasure-house of high culture. It would, after all, not resonate with anything in their own surroundings. It might even cause them to think themselves more important than they really were. Consequently, generation after generation of State schools have concentrated their attention on the so-called 'core subjects' - English, maths, science, history, geography - plus a certain number of non-subjects like P.E., religion, and its secular counterpart, personal and social education.

They have never asked themselves whether these things are valuable in themselves to the individual children who have to wade through them. They are part of the essential mechanism by which we create the next generation of people who will do as they are told and learn what is good for them.

Russell was a fine writer and possibly the most accomplished mathematician of his time. He did not, however, see either writing or mathematics as things which needed to be thrust down children's throats. He wanted England to become the sort of classless society which he thought post-revolutionary Russia was starting to be. It is easy for us, with the benefit of hindsight, to laugh behind our hands at what was undoubtedly a misunderstanding of what was going on in the Soviet Union. Russell's basic desire was a noble one: for all children to have free access to the whole of knowledge, and the right to take into their minds any part of it that excited them or which they saw as useful. He wanted no-one to go through life convinced that only certain bits of learning were right for them.

This is not to say that Russell rejected the idea of a curriculum, and even of an 'essential' element in learning. His own intellect, formed outside the classroom, could not easily accept the idea that it could ever be 'boring' to learn. He had always been intrigued by knowledge of all kinds, and hoped that by right teaching-methods even the least conventionally 'academic' pupils could be induced to acquire it. He wanted learning to be congenial to children from all backgrounds, and could see no way of attaining that goal other than the systematic presentation of ideas from as many different parts of human knowledge as possible. He accepted that his own preferred study, mathematics, would not appeal to every child:

> "A few boys and girls like geometry and algebra, but the great majority do not. I doubt if this is wholly due to faulty methods in teaching. A sense for mathematics, like musical capacity, is mainly a gift of the gods, and I believe it to be quite rare, even in a moderate degree. Nevertheless, every boy and girl should have a taste of mathematics, in order to discover those who have a talent for it."
>
> (On Education, p.177)

This is a long way from the present National Curriculum, whose subjects are not merely introduced to children to allow them to make informed choices. Instead, it compels all children to spend unconscionable amounts of time and often frustrated attention on learning things which they will never use, and clearly have no interest in, long, long after they have finished 'tasting' them. This leads, as Russell realised that it would, to a reinforcement of the baleful 'class' system. Based as it is on the cultural and intellectual preoccupations of the middle and upper classes, our National Curriculum, in its present form, convinces millions of youngsters every year that they are not part of the same culture as their teachers, and the more privileged of their schoolmates. They often react to this feeling by adopting an aggressively 'Philistine' approach to any learning which they see as 'posh'. Quite commonly, they underline this rejection of the school and its ways by ganging up on pupils who try to profit from their schooling by working hard and doing what their teachers tell them to do.

At the end of this process, when young people have received their education, and derived from it whatever profit they are able to, in the form of career opportunities and a more or less enjoyable way of life, Russell perceived that they were always likely to be judged not only by the amount of raw knowledge that they might possess, but also according to a pernicious, arbitrary and class-based pseudo-moral valuation:

> *"Wherever unjust inequalities exist, a man who profits by them tends to protect himself from a sense of guilt by theories suggesting that he is in some way better than those who are less fortunate."*

(Education and the Social Order, p.99)

The expansion of comprehensive education has undermined, to a limited extent, the old conviction that only high culture and the sort of learning that gives entree to highly-paid professions can be thought of as valuable, and that only those who possess it can truly claim to be 'worthy', in the most exalted moral sense. Yet we still, as a nation, tend to think of youngsters who appear to be devoting themselves to school study as 'good', and those who reject it, or try to pursue their own lines of thought as 'bad' or 'disruptive'. Children who meekly submit to the academic curriculum and show themselves to be enthusiastic about the same things as their teachers are most often accorded the highest praise and the best rewards that a school can give. We still use the words 'good' and 'bad' to describe children's success or failure at their various school studies: one boy is 'good' at French, another is 'bad' at maths. We never seem to reflect that if the primary reference of words such as 'good' and 'bad' is a moral one, we are subtly teaching children that even if they avoid doing things which are recognisably 'wrong' in the moral sense, they can still fail in that sphere by not succeeding at school. It is remarkable that when young people break the Law, and reports have to be drawn up in order to decide what shall be done with them, an important part of the information which is collected about them concerns their schooling. Failure in class may well be one of the factors which the Court will consider as having a direct bearing on their behaviour. A Judge may order a young person to show that they are improving in their general moral disposition by 'working harder' at school.

Class distinctions, then, are likely to be sustained by an education system which receives its defining characteristics from the belief that some studies are always more worthwhile, more socially and morally valuable than others. My old Teacher Training College, St. Mark and St. John, had as its motto 'Abeunt studia in Mores', which means something like 'Studies mould Character'. There was a time when I believed that, and held that to learn anything was likely to improve one's general behaviour. I cannot say that I ever worked out exactly how this could happen, but I certainly felt that it was true. After all, did not my own studies make me feel Middle Class, and identify me with the supervisors and the organisers of this world? Russell, I think, would have challenged me on this, and suggested that only study which engaged my whole-hearted enthusiasm, and enabled me to live a more productive life, at whatever level I was best suited to, could be called valid.

Russell and patriotism

Russell lived through a time in which the nature and purpose of patriotic sentiment changed subtly but radically. He was born into a world in which English people absorbed love of their native land with their mother's milk. The great majority of his contemporaries would, if asked, have insisted that to be British was to draw the winning ticket in life's lottery. Even the poor, who received little in the way of positive benefit from the greatness of their motherland, reacted to socialist and internationalist ideas far less energetically than their continental brothers and sisters. The adult generation among which Russell was brought up included aged people who had themselves stood with Wellington at Waterloo, under officers many of whom had bought their commissions. Many of them carried on their backs the marks of almost unimaginably brutal floggings. Those who had been sailors could recount how their captains had laid their ships alongside those of republican France and smashed them to matchwood. They were used to poverty and suffering, and accepted that they owed everything to their sovereign and country.

In this antique world, war was a normal part of political life. Clausewitz's dictum, that war is politics carried on by different means, was completely understood. In any case, wars were generally manageable, consisting mainly of a series of battles lasting little more than a day, fought between ranks of professional soldiers within a confined space. Civilians suffered when enemy armies trampled across their territory, but anyone who was not in the immediate neighbourhood of a battle might be forgiven for thinking themselves more or less safe from the dangers of war. Napoleon had foreshadowed a more universal type of war by taking his armies into other parts of Europe and trying to establish French rule there. Yet after his defeat, in an essentially pre-modern battle, it was almost a century before anything like his style of campaigning scarred the Continent again.

Russell lived long enough to see a new style of war. It was a war of whole peoples, in which generations of young men were conscripted, without any consideration of their private taste for soldiering or their belief in the cause for which they were compelled to fight, and sent into a vast killing machine. In its maw they saw and did unconscionable things, and were wounded or killed by other young men who were themselves forced to fight anyone who wore a different uniform from theirs.

As he saw the infernal stupidity of the first World War unfolding in front of him, Russell realised that it could only happen because the people of the belligerent nations had all been taught that the men who governed their homeland knew better than them what was good for them. They had learned to accept without comment or criticism the idea that their individual lives meant nothing except in the transcendent perspective of the life of the Nation.

He commented tartly on the hypocrisy which afflicts rulers when they try to explain to the world why they are sending their armies into other peoples' countries:

> *"When, for example, the Transvaal was found to contain gold, the British invaded it. Lord Salisbury assured the nation that 'we seek no goldfields'. But somehow or other we happened to go where the goldfields were, and to find ouselves in possession of them at the end of the war."*
>
> (Education and the Social Order, p.86)

and,

> *"To take another illustration: everybody knows that the British went to Southern Persia from a desire to benefit the Southern Persians, but it is doubtful whether we should have taken so much interest in their welfare if they had not inhabited a country full of oil."*
>
> (Education and the Social Order, p.86.)

In short, all foreign policy is about the interests of the State. Anything else is peripheral and can be jettisoned at a moment's notice if necessary. Yet every generation, as it grows up, seems to approve, and want to see those who come after it subjected to, the very system of education which produces this barren and dangerous disposition to pursue the aggrandisement of the nation. As Russell put it:

> *"Throughout the Western world boys and girls are taught that their most important social loyalty is to the State of which they are citizens, and that their duty to the State is to act as its government may direct. Lest they question this doctrine, they are taught false history, false politics, false economics. They are informed of the misdeeds of foreign States, but not of the misdeeds of their own State ... They are taught to believe that when, contrary to expectation, their own country does conquer some foreign country, it does so in order to spread civilisation, or the light of the Gospel, or a lofty moral tone, or prohibition, or something else which is equally noble."*
>
> (Education and the Social Order, p.83)

Many parents and teachers would probably add *"and a damn good thing too"*. We still behave as if we thought that obedience to Authority - even oppressive and arbitrary Authority, so long as it is in some way 'ours' - is always laudable, because we are British, and therefore act from the best possible motives in everything we do. We value conformity in our children, and remind them of how important we believe it is every time we impose on schools courses in 'citizenship', or 'personal and social education'.

Nowadays, these courses tend to have in them an element of sensitivity training and pseudo-democratic discourse, but - and I speak with experience of using them - they are ultimately about curbing young people's self-expression, and training them in submitting to a benevolent dictatorship. We say that we are teaching them to make good, adult decisions in their future lives, to treat all their fellows with respect, and to become good, law-abiding adults.

Yet this teaching is still essentially 'pedagogical'. It presupposes that the teacher, because he or she is a teacher, is entitled to prescribe and limit the ideas which pupils take in and go on to express. Radical notions, including anarchism, self-regulation, rejection of the oppressive aspects of schooling or atheism would not be allowed to divert the pupils' attention from the set ideas of the lesson. These would, no doubt, be 'positive', 'life-affirming', 'multicultural' and liberal, in harmony with the spirit of the times, but they would do nothing to set the children free from the basic ground-rules of life in a school: that teacher knows best, and deserves to be obeyed.

Russell blamed this dogged pursuit of conformity on the teaching of patriotism in schools. We no longer openly encourage children to devote themselves to Queen and Country, as we did when I was a child, and celebrated Empire Day with all the usual claptrap about how wonderful it was to have countries all over the world subject to our rule. Yet the heartbeat of irrational pride in the mere fact of being British is still strong, and it leads us to feel that we are making some enormous concession when we include the languages and customs of our immigrant citizens in our teaching programmes. We still worry that we might be harbouring amongst us large numbers of people who do not actually accept the structures of our national life: people, in short, who can not be relied on in a crisis.

Although the details of our imposed cultural presuppositions have changed somewhat, we still expect schools to mould our young in conformity with them. As Russell noticed in his day, States do what they can compel their people to do. Schools, because they are seen as an arm of the State, and tributary to it, will always strive to produce young adults who can be easily persuaded to collaborate with the policy of the State, whatever that may be.

If the State is fairly enlightened, democratic and civilised, its policy expresses all those virtues. But it cannot allow any substantial number of its people to think entirely for themselves, because if it does, when its policy requires it to do something cynical or uncivilised - like joining in the Vietnam War, or supporting some piece of Real-politik which other States with which it is in alliance are hell-bent on - it will not be able to manipulate public opinion into agreeing with it.

Russell's answer to this problem was a radical one, even by today's standards:

> *"The idea that what is taught to children should, if possible, be true is, I know, very subversive, and in some of its applications even illegal. But I cannot resist the conviction that instruction is better when it teaches truth than when it teaches falsehood. History ought to be taught in exactly the same way in all countries of the world, and history text-books ought to be drawn up by the League of Nations, with an assistant from the United States, and another from Soviet Russia* (that would have been an interesting encounter! C. R. S.). *History should be world history, and should emphasise matters of cultural importance rather than wars. In so far as wars must be taught, they should not be taught only from the point of view of the victor, and of heroic deeds."*
> (Education and the Social Order, p.89)

He wanted to see children equipped to think their own thoughts and come to their own conclusions, relying on their own perceptions, and having the courage, when others seemed determined to do the wrong, disastrous thing because it was popular, to act as their conscience led them. Nowadays, I suspect he would want to see schools encouraging their pupils to demand a stronger voice in making school policy, and particularly in working out ways to deal with racism, bullying, sexual oppression and sexism. He would want them to examine their own little internal 'nationalisms' - the attitudes of boys towards girls, the oppressive treatment of young pupils by older ones, even the arbitrary dominance of teachers over pupils.

Chapter five

The individual and society in Russell's thought

States have always struggled to establish themselves as powerful, unitary entities, whose component individuals always think and act as their designated leaders tell them to. When states are large and powerful they tend to see size and power as good qualities in themselves, conferring on them an unchallengeable prestige, and a prescriptive right to do anything which seems right to them, and call it justice. When I was a boy, back in the 40s and 50s of the last century, I was taught to be proud of the British Empire, because it was big, strong and ours. The people who lived in it, I was told, were all loyal to the British Crown, and thought of England as the 'Home Country'. They all respected white people, if they did not happen to be white themselves, and the few among them who hated their imperial governors were criminals, just like the cat-burglars and muggers whose crimes were recounted in the daily papers. When my primary school teacher taught us about Robert Clive, and his career as the leader of John Company's Army, she did not think it right to point out that both he and his French adversaries were fighting their wars mostly with sepoys, Indian soldiers who had never been consulted about whether they wanted to fight each other under the flags of nations thousands of miles away. The story of the Black Hole of Calcutta was retailed to us as an example of the primitive cruelty which the Empire was sworn to stamp out. We were expected to see it as a full and proper justification for all the brutalities which the Empire meted out to the Indians after the Mutiny, including blowing them from the mouths of cannon, and hanging them in public, after assuring them that their bodies would be disposed of in the way most offensive to their religion. Like most of my contemporaries, I quickly learned that other nations were foreigners, and incapable of acting justly, but we were British, and therefore selected by nature, providence or God, depending on your beliefs about the author of our destiny, to rule.

I have since learned to be appalled by such ideas. I have met people from all over the world, and have come to realise that every culture has strengths and weaknesses, valuable aspects without which the world would be much poorer than it is, and customs which rightly offend decent people everywhere. Britain gave the world Shakespeare, but it should hang its head in shame for its treatment of Ireland. Russell, in his time, also saw that he lived in a nation, which actively discouraged its people from thinking clearly about moral issues when that nation's prestige was in question.

He asserted that:

> *"It has been the custom for education to favour one's own State, one's own religion, the male sex, and the rich. In countries where various religions exist side by side, the State is not able to favour any one of them in its schools, but this has led to the creation of schools belonging to the various sects, or, as in New York City and Boston, to distortion, in the Catholic interest, of the history taught in the public schools."*
> (Education and the Social Order, p.145)

He perceived, as many after him have done, that education, far from being centred on children, has come to be a weapon in the struggle for power between religions, classes, and ultimately nations. By moulding children into docile, unreflective representatives of one social grouping or another, their teachers try to ensure that the children they work with will not singularise themselves, stepping out of the prevailing mores of their community and challenging not only their supremacy, but even their legitimacy. Russell propounds this idea in a striking way:

> *"The pupil is not considered for his own sake, but as a recruit: the educational machine is not concerned with his welfare, but with ulterior political purposes. There is no reason to suppose that the State will ever place the interests of the child before its own interests; we have, therefore, to inquire whether there is any possibility of a State whose interests, where education is concerned, will be approximately identical to those of the child."*
> (Education and the Social Order, p.145)

In Russell's day this process of 'recruitment' had one overriding purpose: to prepare young people to defend whatever the Government considered to be the interests of the State, by being ready to become soldiers in time of war. Therefore, throughout his long life, he tried to eliminate war from the life of the nations. In the early part of the last century he had already seen that some sort of supranational Authority, to which all nations would be subject, would be needed to ensure that whenever political disagreements placed one nation athwart another, there would be a means of settling their differences which was not open war. It is unfortunate that the United Nations has not yet contrived to make war obsolete, to the point where:

> *"There would no longer be any need for Officer Training Corps, or for compulsory military service, or for the teaching of false history. Moral training would no longer have homicide as the apex of a virtuous life, to which everything else leads up. The establishment of an international authority sufficiently strong to impose its settlement of disputes upon recalcitrant states is, I am convinced, the most important reform from an educational as well as from every other point of view."*　　(Education and the Social Order, p.145)

The post-war settlement, however, headed up by the United Nations, has led to a dilution of the military component of education in many countries. Compulsory military service has largely disappeared from Europe, and where it still exists, young people are often allowed to choose to work for society in more socially useful ways if they do not wish to learn to fight. In some countries this alternative service is still regarded as second-rate, and may extend beyond the time allotted to soldiering, but at least young people who reject war as a solution to political differences no longer risk serious and prolonged ill-treatment, as they did in the past.

Having dealt with the baneful influence on young people of the tacit assumption that young men, at least, need to be prepared for war, Russell attacked one of the great maladies of our life, which among many other things, makes easier the task of the militarists - our great love of both conformity and uniformity. His comments on this aspect of society are striking, and not entirely 'politically correct', but they are worth recording for their sheer clarity and lack of inhibition:

> *"I come now to ... a too great love of uniformity. This may
> exist ... both in the bureaucrat and in the herd. Children are
> instinctively hostile to anything 'odd' in other children,
> especially in the ages from ten to fifteen. If the authorities
> realise that this conventionality is undesirable they can guard
> against it in various ways, and they can, as was suggested in
> an earlier chapter, place the cleverer children in separate
> schools. The intolerance of eccentricity that I am speaking of
> is strongest in the stupidest children, who tend to regard the
> peculiar tastes of clever children as affording just grounds
> for persecution. When the authorities are also stupid (which
> can occur) they will tend to side with the stupid children, and
> acquiesce, at least tacitly, in rough treatment for those who
> show intelligence. In that case, a society will be produced in
> which all the important positions will be won by those whose
> stupidity enables them to please the herd. Such a society will
> have corrupt politicians, ignorant schoolmasters, policemen
> who cannot catch criminals, and judges who condemn
> innocent men."*
>
> (Education and the Social Order, pp.147-8)

Could he be talking about our society? Certainly, we seem to have
developed a willingness to attenuate our most liberal ideas with the
brand of discourse which appeals to the readers of tabloid papers
like the 'Sun'. Politicians appear to assume that such people are
unable to think humanely and see even a short distance beyond
their immediate, often brutal, response to social phenomena which
they do not understand. This perception acts as a brake upon social
progress, since it often impels governments to pass illiberal laws
merely to please the herd.

Russell's Beacon Hill School

Good education does not always take place in schools, and the test
of a person's ideas about raising children is not necessarily whether
he can run a school according to them. Russell, however, found
himself compelled to start a school. He had small children and an
urgent need for money, and having decided with Dora, his wife at
the time, that no school existed at the time to which he could with
a clear conscience send his offspring, he decided to start Beacon
Hill School in 1927.

The school was set up in an interesting building, Telegraph House, which Russell rented from his brother. It had been a semaphore station on the South Downs, between Chichester and Petersfield, part of the chain which carried messages between Portsmouth and London. It had handled many of the important messages which announced the progress of the Royal Navy during the Napoleonic Wars, including the news of Nelson's victory at Trafalgar. It was not what modern educationist and inspectors would identify as an ideal building for running a traditional school - Russell called it *"ugly and rather absurd"* - but it was set in a landscape which was superb as a place for children to play, and lose themselves in the beauty of Nature. It offered magnificent views of the Sussex Weald and even the Isle of Wight. From it one could clearly see the liners approaching Southampton. It had no less than two hundred and thirty acres of wild land, with a good mixture of undergrowth, brush, heather and bracken, and virgin forest, full of wild-life, including deer. At the time there were only a few scattered farms a mile distant, and to the East it was possible to follow footpaths over unenclosed land for fifty miles. If schools are about good environments for growing up in freedom and learning to use the body as well as the mind, Telegraph House must have been a demi-Paradise for active youngsters.

Russell faced several problems from the very start. In his Autobiography, he mentions three major ones. The first was the ever-present problem of finance. He was paying his brother a heavy rent, which he had agreed to do in order to prevent the house going to someone outside the family, as well as ensuring that he could use its wonderful surroundings for his school. He could have avoided a financial burden by taking many more children than be wanted to, and altering the school enough to make it attractive to conventional parents, who would, no doubt, have expected him to do all the usual, corrosive things that schoolmasters are in the habit of doing to their pupils. He would also have had to restrict the children's food. Instead, he subsidised the fees he charged with the proceeds from his books and lecture tours. This occupied much of his time, and prevented him from concentrating his efforts on the children.

His second problem was one which most progressive educators face at one time or another. His staff could not be trusted to work according to his ideas about education, unless he happened to be watching them. The abrasive English tradition, which holds that a teacher is a despot in charge of a miniature autocracy, and can do more or less what he likes to control and instruct his or her pupils dies hard, and was still vigorous in those days.

His third problem was, he acknowledged, more serious:

> " ... we got an undue proportion of problem children. We ought to have been on the lookout for this pit-fall, but at first we were glad to take almost any child. The parents who were most inclined to try new methods were those who had difficulties with their children. As a rule, these difficulties were the fault of the parents, and the ill effects of their unwisdom were renewed in each holiday. Whatever may have been the cause, many of the children were cruel and destructive. To let the children go free was to establish a reign of terror, in which the strong kept the weak trembling and miserable. A school is like the world: only government can prevent brutal violence. And so I found myself, when the children were not at lessons, obliged to supervise them continually to stop cruelty."
> (Autobiography, p.389)

Russell did not try to suppress unacceptable behaviour, or pretend it did not exist. His Autobiography does not record that he used the same radically democratic approach as A. S. Neill at Summerhill, putting all issues of social misbehaviour in the hands of a School Meeting, but he certainly tried to find out why it was happening:

> "We divided them into three groups, bigs, middles, and smalls. One of the middles was perpetually ill-treating the smalls, so I asked him why he did it. His answer was: 'The bigs hit me, so I hit the smalls; that's fair.' And he really thought it was."   (Autobiography, p389)

It may be surmised that Russell's own upbringing, away from the experience of 'normal' schooling, hid from him the psychological insight which Neill perceived clearly, that children in groups respond unconsciously to the collective pressure of their peers, and can only learn to manage the fears and frustrations which that pressure produces if they have a right to assert that they are themselves a component part of their peer-group, and as such entitled to its protection from the caprice of its other members. He does not mention group-meetings and democratic forms in his own account of Beacon Hill, and although he laid stress on the pedagogy of freedom and a child-centred approach, he did not seem to want to hand over to the children the large areas of autonomy which Neill accorded to his pupils at Summerhill.

Russell knew of Neill's work, and the two men wrote to each other warmly when Neill was frustrated in his attempts to persuade the Ministry of Education, where Russell had influence, to allow him to employ a Frenchman to teach French. There is no doubt that Russell found himself in the same general field of thought as Neill, and respected his work and attitude to children. In a letter to him Neill pointed out the differences which still existed between the home-educated aristocrat and the maverick dominie:

> "I marvel that two men, working from different angles, should arrive at essentially the same conclusions. Your book and mine are complimentary. It may be that the only difference between us comes from our respective complexes. I observe that you say little or nothing about handwork in education. My hobby has always been handwork, and where your child asks you about stars my pupils ask me about steels and screw-threads. Possibly I attach more importance to emotion in education than you do." (Autobiography, p.419)

Certainty, Russell never freed himself from the visceral conviction that education, though concerned with more than the intellect, could not be discussed without close reference to the acquisition of ideas and facts. Whether that is a major fault or a good reason for commendation depends upon one's own standpoint. It is clear from the little which has come down to us about the regime at Beacon Hill that Russell tried to do far more than simply instruct. He and his wife strove to build healthy minds in healthy bodies.

He remained unsatisfied with his efforts:

> "In retrospect, I feel that several things were mistaken in the principles upon which the school was conducted. Young children in a group cannot be happy without a certain amount of order and routine. Left to amuse themselves, they are bored, and turn to bullying or destruction. In their free time, there should always be an adult to suggest some agreeable game or amusement, and to supply an initiative which is hardly to be expected of young children."
> (Autobiography, p.390)

Neill would have disagreed with him. For some reason the Scots dominie felt more at ease with children during what he called their 'bandit stage' than the philosopher, who seems to have been disturbed by the unfettered play of youthful energy. Russell may be forgiven, however, by those who feel that forgiveness is due, because he did, at least, recognise a serious weakness in the practice of education by those who say that they believe in freedom for children:

> *"Another thing that was wrong was that there was a pretence of more freedom than in fact existed. There was very little freedom where health and cleanliness were concerned. The children had to wash, to clean their teeth, and to go to bed at the right time. True, we had never professed that there should be freedom in such matters, but foolish people, and especially journalists in search of a sensation, had said or believed that we advocated a complete absence of all restraints and compulsions. The older children, when told to brush their teeth, would sometimes say sarcastically: 'Call this a free school!' Those who had heard their parents talking about the freedom to be expected in the school would test it by seeing how far they could go in naughtiness without being stopped. As we only forbade things that were obviously harmful, such experiments were apt to be very inconvenient."*
>
> (Autobiography, p.390)

Postscript

Another person whose status invests his opinions with significance, if not authority, wrote a book which appeared recently to a fanfare of conflicting opinions. Chris Woodhead, the former Chief Inspector of Schools, used it to direct a salvo of bile against modern ideas about education. He had, he insisted tried 'modern methods' of education during his callow youth as an English teacher, and they had not 'worked'. I imagine Russell would have wanted to examine that assertion a little more closely, in the light of the fact that many of Woodhead's contemporaries had certainly found child-centred approaches to teaching both enriching and enjoyable. But Woodhead had been Chief Inspector, and therefore expected the exclusive deference which the English still accord to Senior Intellectuals when they pronounce on such high matters as the organisation of schools.

His critique of the schools he had been charged to oversee boiled down to a few simple assertions: the Government needed to be stricter, more prescriptive, less tolerant of experiment, and more determined to expel from the teaching profession anyone who could not or would not implement their programme. He saw no need for research. He had already stigmatised all organised examination of the teaching process by University based academics as little better than the Black Arts. He would have dismissed Russell's writings as idealistic rubbish. Just as the Inner Party in Orwell's '1984' would have replaced the entire text of the 'Declaration of Independence' with the single word 'Thoughtcrime', so Woodhead saw no reason to spend any time at all thinking any thoughts other than his own about the nation's schools, and deeming any ideas which clashed with his own to be 'rubbish'. Such simplistic rhetoric has always found an open ear in Britain, because as a nation we tend to cleave to the 'no nonsense' style of working, fearing the intellect as a foreign, and therefore suspicious, preoccupation.

I mention Woodhead at the conclusion of this book only because I fear that if as a nation we choose his ideas as a basis for our education system we shall fail to overcome in the 21st Century the enormous errors which allowed the products of our schools to blunder so tragically in the 20th. Only humanistic, respectful, and above all thoroughly meditated education, offered in a rich environment by wise and kindly people who have defeated their own internal demons and can be quiet while the children play round them, can assure us a brighter future.

Bibliography

Holmes, Edmond (1911) *What Is and What Might Be*, London: Constable and Co. Ltd.

Park, Joe (1964) *Bertrand Russell on Education*, London: George Allen and Unwin

Russell, Bertrand, (1916) *Principles of Social Reconstruction*, London: George Allen and Unwin

Russell, Bertrand (1926) *On Education, especially in early Childhood*, London: George Allen and Unwin

Russell, Bertrand (1932) *Education and the Social Order*, London: George Allen and Unwin

Russell, Bertrand, (1949) *Authority and the Individual*, London; George Allen and Unwin

Russell, Bertrand, (1950) *Unpopular Essays*, London: George Allen and Unwin

Russell, Bertrand (1951) *New Hopes for a Changing World*, London; George Allen and Unwin

Russell, Bertrand, (1954) *Human Society in Ethics and Politics*, London: George Allen and Unwin

Russell, Bertrand (1975*) Mortals and Others: American Essays 1931-1935*, London: George Allen and Unwin.

Russell, Bertrand (1975*) The Autobiography of Bertrand Russell*, London: George Allen and Unwin.
Single Volume ISBN 0 04 921022 x

Shute, Chris (1993) *Compulsory Schooling Disease*, Nottingham; Educational Heretics Press

Selected Russell Quotations

CODES

OE = *On Education*
ESO = *Education and the Social Order*
PSR = *Principles of Social Reconstruction*
HSEP = *Human Society in Ethics and Politics*
UE = *Unpopular Essays*
AI = *Authority and the Individual*
NHCW = *New Hopes for a Changing World*

The prevention of free inquiry is unavoidable so long as the purpose of education is to produce belief rather than thought, to compel the young to hold positive opinions on doubtful matters rather than let them see the doubtfulness and be encouraged to independence of mind. Education ought to foster the wish for the truth, not the conviction that some particular creed is the truth. But it is creeds that hold men together in fighting organisations: Churches, States, political parties. It is intensity of belief in a creed that produces efficiency in fighting: victory comes to those who feel the strongest certainty about matters on which doubt is the only rational attitude.   (PSR p.107)

We must have some concept of the kind of person we wish to produce before we can have any definite opinion as to the education which we consider best.   (OE p.28)

We are faced with the paradoxical fact that education has become one of the chief obstacles to intelligence and freedom of thought.
(OE p.28)

The spontaneous wish to learn, which every normal child possesses, as shown in its efforts to walk and talk, should be the driving force in education.   (OE p.25)

The trouble with the world is that the stupid are cocksure and the intelligent full of doubt.   (OE p.25)

The wish to preserve the past rather than the hope of creating the future dominates the minds of those who control the teaching of the young.   (OE p.25)

Happiness in childhood is absolutely necessary to the production of the best type of human being.   (OE p.25)

If curiosity is to be fruitful, it must be associated with a certain technique for the acquisition of knowledge. There must be habits of observation, belief in the possibility of knowledge, patience and industry.   (OE p.43)

The sum of human knowledge and the complexity of human problems are perpetually increasing; therefore every generation must overhaul its educational methods if time is to be found for what is new.   (OE p.20)

There must be in the world many parents who, like the present author, have young children whom they are anxious to educate as well as possible, but reluctant to expose to the evils of existing educational institutions.   (OE p.7)

In universities, mathematics is taught mainly to men who are going to teach mathematics to men who are going to teach mathematics to men ... Sometimes, it is true, there is an escape from this treadmill. Archimedes used mathematics to kill Romans, Galileo to improve the Grand Duke of Tuscany's artillery, modern physicists (grown more ambitious) to exterminate the human race. It is usually on this account that the study of mathematics is commended to the general public as worthy of State support.
                    (HSEP p.54)

Some 'Advanced Thinkers' are of the opinion that anyone who differs from the conventional opinion must be in the right. This is a delusion; if it were not, truth would be easier to come by than it is. There are infinite possibilities of error, and more cranks take up unfashionable errors than unfashionable truths.   (UE p.91)

... so long as men are not trained to withhold judgment in the absence of evidence, they will be led astray by cocksure prophets, and it likely that the leaders will be either ignorant fanatics or dishonest charlatans. To endure uncertainty is difficult, but then so are most of the other virtues.   (UE p.32)

A boy will toil uphill with a toboggan for the sake of a few brief moments of bliss during the descent; no one has to urge him to be industrious, and however he may puff and pant he is still happy.

(AI p.51)

If you think your belief is based upon reason, you will support it by argument, rather than by persecution, and will abandon it if the argument goes against you. But if your belief is based on faith, you will realise that argument is useless, and will therefore resort to force either in the form of persecution or by stunting and distorting the minds of the young in what is called 'education'. This last is peculiarly dastardly, since it takes advantage of the defencelessness of immature minds. Unfortunately it is practised in a greater or less degree in the schools of every civilised country.

(HSEP p.220)

..there can be no agreement between those who regard education as a means of instilling certain definite beliefs, and those who think that it should produce the power of independent judgment.

(OE p.8)

The opinions of parents are immensely important, because, for lack of expert knowledge, parents are too often a drag upon the best educationalists. (OE p.8)

...we must approach educational democracy carefully, so as to destroy in the process as little as possible of the valuable products that happen to have been associated with social injustice.

(OE p.14)

...the right discipline consists, not in external compulsion, but in habits of mind which lead spontaneously to desirable rather than undesirable activities. (OE p.22)

The fact is that children are not naturally either 'good' or 'bad'. They are born with only reflexes and a few instincts; out of these, by the action of the environment, habits are produced, which may be either healthy or morbid. (OE p.25)

...much of what passes for knowledge at any given time is likely to be more or less mistaken, but... the mistakes can be rectified by care and industry. (OE p.30)

The administrator of the future must be the servant of free citizens, not the benevolent ruler of admiring subjects.   (OE p.32)

The teacher should love his children better than his State or his Church; otherwise he is not an ideal teacher.   (OE p.33)

.. with the death of curiosity we may reckon that active intelligence, also, has died.   (OE p.44)

All sorts of intellectual systems - Christianity, Socialism, Patriotism etc., - are ready, like orphan asylums, to give safety in return for servitude. A free mental life cannot be as warm and comfortable and sociable as a life enveloped in a creed. (OE p.44)

The way is clear. Do we love our children enough to take it? Or shall we let them suffer as we have suffered? Shall we let them be twisted and stunted and terrified in youth, to be killed afterwards in futile wars which their intelligence was too cowed to prevent? A thousand ancient fears obstruct the road to happiness and freedom.
     (OE p.171)

The first thing the average educator sets to work to kill in the young is imagination.   Imagination is lawless, undisciplined, individual, and neither correct nor incorrect; in all these respects it is inconvenient to the teacher, especially when competition requires a rigid order of merit.   (ESO p.95)

If personal quality is to be preserved, definite teaching must be reduced to a minimum, and criticism must never be carried to such lengths as to produce timidity in self-expression.   But these maxims are not likely to lead to work that will be pleasing to an inspector.   (ESO p.96)

... much education consists in the instilling of unfounded dogmas in the place of a spirit of inquiry.   This results, not necessarily from any fault in the teacher, but from a curiculum which demands too much apparent knowledge, with a consequent need of haste and undue definiteness.   (ESO p.99)

The tendency of those who construct a curriculum without having experience of teaching is to put too much into it, with the result that nothing is learned thoroughly.   (ESO p.101)

Arithmetic ... is overvalued; in British elementary schools it takes up far more of the time than it should. The average man should be able to do accounts, but beyond that he will seldom have occasion for sums. What he may have learnt of complicated arithmetic will be of no more practical use to him in later life that would the amount of Latin he could have learnt in the same time, and of far less use than what he could have learnt of anatomy, physiology and elementary hygiene.   (ESO p.102)

Competition is not only bad as an educational fact, but also as a ideal to be held before the young. What the world now needs is not competition but organisation and co-operation; all belief in the utility of competition has become an anachronism. ... the emotions connected with it are the emotions of hostility and ruthlessness. The conception of society as an organic whole is very difficult for those whose minds have been steeped in competitive ideas. Ethically, therefore, no less than economically, it is undesirable to teach the young to be competitive.   (ESO p.104)

Readers may remember Pavlov's dog, who learnt to distinguish ellipses from circles. But as Pavlov gradually made the ellipses more nearly circular, there came at last a point - where the ratio of major and minor axes was 9.8 - at which the dog's powers of discrimination gave way ... The same sort of thing happens to many boys and girls in school. If they are compelled to tackle problems that are definitely beyond their powers, a kind of bewildered terror seizes hold of them, not only in relation to the particular problem in question, but also as regards all intellectually neighbouring territory.   Many people are bad at mathematical subjects all their lives because they started them too young. Arithmetic and mathematics generally are learnt at too early an age, with the result that in regard to them, many pupils acquire the artificial stupidity of Pavlov's canine student of geometry.
                    (ESO p.97)

Shakespeare did not write with a view to boring school children; he wrote to with a view to delighting his audiences. If he does not give you delight, you had better ignore him.
                    (NHCW, quoted in *Bertrand Russell's Best* (1958)
                    R. E. Egner, p.87)